ESPECIALLY FOR THE YOUNG PREACHER

By
Dennis P. Wiggs

Ministering to the Family
Personal Financial Suggestions
Church Programs
Forms for Church Ministry

Copyright 2016
By
Dennis P. Wiggs

ISBN 978-1-940609-54-6
Soft Cover

All rights reserved.
No part of this book may be reproduced or transmitted in any form or by any means, electronic or mechanical, including photocopying, recording, or by any information storage and retrieval system, without permission in writing from the copyright owner.
The exception would be the forms.

The book was printed in the United State of America.

To order additional copies of this book contact

denniswiggs@gmail.com

FWB
For Worthwhile Books Publications
Columbus, Ohio

INTRODUCTION

I trusted Christ as my personal Savior at age 15. At age 16, I sensed the call to the ministry. By reading I and II Timothy in the quietness of my upstairs bedroom, that call was confirmed through prayer to Almighty God. After announcing my call to preach God's Word, I soon went to youth camp at Black Mountain, NC. Hearing that I had announced plans to preach, the youth camp director, Lloyd Ballard, asked me to speak during the Thursday night service. I preached all I knew in just a few minutes. During the invitation, Mrs. Gertrude Ballard led the young people in singing an invitational chorus. Quite a few youth went to the altar to accept Jesus Christ as Savior. That evening the girl I was dating, Betty Craft, was led to pray "the sinner's prayer" by camper R. J. Kennedy. It was an evening of great rejoicing.

When I went back to Smithfield, NC, my pastor, Chester Phillips, encouraged other preachers to invite Dennis Wiggs to preach. Opportunities to minister God's Word were provided. I began Wednesday morning prayer sessions in my church before school opened. (The church was across the street from the school). My home church employed me to serve as youth director during the next summer.

As a young preacher, I immediately sought guidance in preparing to preach God's Word. The writings of Pastor J. C. Griffin's magazine articles were read, studied, and filed in a small box.

As a student at Bob Jones University, I was privileged to take subjects on church administration by Dr. James Bellis. Classes under Dr. Walter Fremont presented practical instructions on how to live effectively in this life. At Columbia Bible College Graduate School, I received simple Bible teachings by Professor James Hatch that led me to practical Christianity in my life.

While ministering in Williamsburg, Virginia, articles began to develop on the different subjects you will find in this book. Dr. Jack Williams provided me the opportunity to publish the articles in *Contact* magazine. Secretary Carol Olds and English teacher Martha Anderson assisted me in preparing the book for printing by Randall House Publications. The enclosed material has been tested in five churches in forty-five years.

Our daughter, Audra Wiggs Kite, prepared the material for the second printing.

My dear wife, Betty Craft Wiggs, has been the inspiration to me for applying the principles in this book. Trusting Christ as Savior at age 15, she soon felt called to serve Christ as a minister's wife. Her degree in education from Bob Jones University prepared her to teach in Christian schools, minister God's Word in Sunday School and other church classes, and help train our five children in the ways of the Lord. This book is dedicated to Betty.

Table of Contents

The Family
    Love Your Valentine 11
    Your Best Friend Should Be Your Wife 15
    The Young Preacher's Wife 19
    The Challenge Of Being The Young Preacher's Mate 23
    The Children And Their Money 27
    Say "Thank You" 31
    Gifts From Church Members 35

Personal Finances
    Plans For The New Year 39
    Set Goals 43
    Pay For A Car 47
    Read Three Books At A Time 51
    Should A Young Preacher Have A Will? 53
    Taxes 57
    Try To Lead Your Church Financially 61
    Your Library 65
    Have A Garden 69
    Pray For Missionaries 71
    How To Make Your Clothes Last Longer 73
    The Young Preacher's Health 75
    Practice Frugality 77
    Preparing For The Future 81
    Financial Principles From Proverbs 85
    Death, Disability And Some Other D's You Must Consider 89
    Remembering 93

The Church
- Be Organized 99
- Your Daily Bible Reading 103
- A Daily Prayer Schedule 107
- When You Move To A New Pastorate 111
- Your First Months At A New Pastorate 115
- Type And File Your Sermons 119
- Your Sermon Material 123
- Sermon Resources 127
- The Lifestyle Of The Young Preacher 131
- The Young Preacher's Appearance 135
- Ministerial Ethics 139
- Keep Your Mouth Shut! 143
- Confidentiality 147
- Getting Eight Men To Do The Work 151
- Ministering From The Vehicle 155
- Go Soul Winning Every Day 157
- Major On Witnessing 161
- Establish A Church Around Men 165
- How To Be A Blessing To Church Members 169
- Your Relationship With The Women's Organizations 171
- Think, Brother, Think 173
- Ministering To Your Church Family 177
- Decisions A Young Preacher Must Face ... 181
- Be A Friend To Preachers 183
- The Church Bulletin 187
- Some Ways To Improve The Mid-Week Services 191
- Hospital Visitation 195
- When You Are Invited To Preach At Another Church 199
- Love Your Congregation 203

Recognize Church Members' Birthdays... 207
Encourage Missionaries via E-Mail 211
The Prayer Meeting 215
Don't Rob Your Church Members Of A
Blessing 219
Should You Conduct A Radio Broadcast? 223
Should I Establish A Christian School?..... 227
Operating A Church School 231
How To Treat The Guest Preacher 235
How To Conduct A Business Meeting 239
Make Missionary Conference A Blessing 243
What If You're Voted Out?............................ 247
How To Leave A Pastorate 251

Forms
Use Forms... 257
Marriage Questionnaire 261
Baptismal Form 265
Request For Funds 266
Church Family Information 268
Information When I Die 269
Child Dedication.. 270

THE FAMILY

LOVE YOUR VALENTINE

February is the month of the Valentine. More candy and flowers will be given that month than at any time of the year. Maybe even the young preacher will "break down" and purchase a box of candy or a few flowers for his mate.

However, the display of love for the bride should not be limited to just one day in February. The young preacher should demonstrate his love and appreciation regularly. If any husband ought to prove his love for his wife, surely it ought to be the young preacher. The woman in the parsonage is a special person. She has followed her preacher-husband to a church where everyone is usually a stranger. The pastor's wife has set up housekeeping in a strange land, and accepted her mate's ministry as her ministry.

The young preacher can take his dear wife for granted. He can be busy ministering to all of the church members and forget the queen of the manse. Let me make some suggestions to benefit the relationship between the preacher and his wife.

Recognize The Position Of The Mate
The young preacher's wife often has few close

friends. Maybe her day is restricted to the home rearing the children, counseling a distraught church member, and keeping the house clean for those unexpected guests. Quite a challenge! "A woman's work is never done, from dawn to setting sun," my wife has reminded me many times. While the preacher-husband is visiting the church members or eating at a restaurant with a pastor friend, the dear wife is "holding the fort."

Love The Mate

Touch her tenderly every day. A woman needs that husbandly affection. Maybe a short neck massage after the evening meal or holding hands while watching the evening news will provide a greater sense of marital security. Take a walk down the street or another safe place.

Tell her "I love you." Those are magic words to a woman who has heard crying, demanding children all day or worked in a job of continued pressure.

Take her out to eat about once a week. (Choose a reasonably priced restaurant.) Arrange for a baby sitter. Spend this profitable time together to reinforce the marital covenant.

Trust your wife. Sharing your prayer requests and then praying together will develop a greater trust and devotion.

Turn your eye away from other women. Adore the one God gave you. Purchase your mate a dress and some perfume. Dress the queen like a queen!

Help The Mate

The young preacher's ministry would be enhanced if the wife could stay home. Everyone would benefit if mother cleaned the house, washed the clothes, prepared the meals, sent the children off to school and met them when they returned home, conducted personal devotions each day at the same time, and sustained a peaceful atmosphere. In other words, be the full-time queen of the manse.

However, if the wife works outside of the home, the husband is obligated to assist the wife. Most women want to wash the dishes, vacuum the floor, dust the furniture, etc. The home is her castle. However, occasionally the young preacher should take over the mop, grab the wash rag, and plug up the vacuum cleaner to relieve the tired wife who has worked all day in the secular world. At least clean the shoes before entering the house!

Assist In Rearing The Children

Yes, it is important to speak to the deacon who has a suggestion, shake hands with the visitors, meet with the church board, or even pray at the altar with someone who just heard your message. But, this should not be the time for the preacher's children to crawl under the pews, run around the parking lot, climb the tree, kick some adult, or pick a fight with another kid. Many wonderful sermons are destroyed by the young preacher's children. An understanding between the preacher, the wife, and the children must be determined before ever going into the church sanctuary. Better to load up the vehicle and go home, leaving the deacon talking, rather than giving the church members something to gossip about the rest of the week.

And, young preacher, hold that baby God gave you and your wife, even if the child does burp on your new suit. Calmly correct your child who is climbing over the church pew. Know what those kids of yours are doing. Remember the young preacher's first responsibility is to the wife and children. The obligation to corral all of the kids is not just the job of the wife.

Something Special On The Un-special Day
Birthdays and anniversaries ought to be recognized, of course. However, a sweet note on the mirror of the bathroom cabinet or on the coffee pot will provide a loving challenge for the new day. The young preacher would do well to call the wife at home once or twice a day just to say "I love you." Both husband and wife should work on new ways to express the growing love between life-long partners. Love the church members as people who need you. But love the wife as someone who is part of your flesh, your ministry, and your fruitfulness. Make her your valentine every day.

YOUR BEST FRIEND SHOULD BE YOUR WIFE

The one who understands you better than anyone else is probably your wife. She sees you when you are encouraged and when you are down. The spouse observes your true outward appearance. The one who married you for better or worse lives with the real you. She doesn't first respect you as pastor, but as husband. She should be your best friend.

A pastor does not have a pastor. Often the wife provides his spiritual guidance. She patiently listens when no one else will bother. She will try to understand the burdens of the ministry when you cannot share them with another person. You can trust her to pray for you. Her counsel is valuable. She is your wife, a very precious woman indeed.

Your Wife May Help Your Ministry Fail Or Succeed

The queen of the parsonage holds a tremendous grip on the life of the preacher. She can help to make him or break him. That is why it is just as important that she be called to the ministry. I met Betty at Cragmont Assembly in Black Mountain, North Carolina. She trusted Christ as Savior the night I preached my first sermon. In that ten-minute sermon, all I knew was preached at least twice. Gertrude ("Ma Ballard," we called her) gave the invitation. As Betty grew in the grace and knowledge of the Lord, He "called" her to be a preacher's wife. Without her encouragement, patience, toleration, and daily praying, where would I be today?

Date Your Mate
At least once a week give her your undivided attention at a restaurant. Hire a babysitter. Schedule this date just as you would any other appointment. When church members want your counsel or assistance during that special time, tell them you have an important appointment. Request to meet them at another time.

It does not require an expensive restaurant with the lights dimmed. Maybe an early morning breakfast or a luncheon special will suffice. A picnic might be sufficient.

Listen To Your Mate
Usually in the evening when the children are asleep is an ideal time to give your spouse fifteen to thirty minutes of your devoted attention. If she has run the house like a drill sergeant all day, she needs to share life's joys, burdens, and plans with her partner. Let her vent her feelings without your interruption.

Give Her Affection
Your wife needs to feel your tender touch of love. A peck on the cheek, a loving touch on the shoulder, a smile of understanding, a back rub while she washes the dishes, or a kiss of appreciation after she prepares a delicious meal. She needs the attention that only you can give. Remember, she also lives in a glass house. Probably

she does not have a close, female friend that she can honestly share her innermost feelings. Your daily affection can help sustain this woman of the manse.

Surprise Her

Surely on her birthday and your anniversary, you will buy her flowers or take her to a nice restaurant or at least send a lovely card. But, surprise her with a special gift on an "un-special" day. Most women love flowers. Spend a few dollars every now and then on your most valuable possession. Think! When you are shopping, ask yourself what you could buy for that dear one that would surprise her. It doesn't have to cost a lot. Just the surprise will overshadow the cost.

Write Her Notes

Anonymous, unkind notes may be delivered to a preacher's wife. Oh, how this hurts. Just as bad is the fact that most of those in the congregation never write kind, considerate notes to the wife of the pastor. Brother, you can fill that void with encouraging notes. Place a love note on her coffee cup. Express your appreciation for her with a poem taped to her bathroom mirror. If she is traveling without you, pin a note on her clothes in the suitcase or travel bag. Never lose that youthful excitement of pleasing the one God has given you.

Contact Her Via Telephone

When I was in graduate school, Professor Frank Sells would use the pay telephone in the hall beside my dorm door to call his wife each afternoon. Oh, what love talk! Unashamedly and loudly, he expressed his love via telephone. Even though he saw her that morning and he would be home in an hour or two, you would have

thought that their absence from each other had been for days.

Just a short telephone call from the study to say "I love you" can do wonders for a marital relationship. When on a trip a call to the home can provide comfort and assurance to a wife who is keeping the home fires burning.

Court The Wife
The day is coming when all of the children will move out and establish their own homes. Don't let this catch you and your mate off guard. Date your mate all of the years the children are growing up. Then, when they leave the nest, you and your queen will still know how to enjoy each other's presence. She is more important to you than the children. Remember, you two are one flesh. The ending years can be even more exciting than the beginning years.

THE YOUNG PREACHER'S WIFE

What a wonderful privilege to serve as the wife of a young preacher! His calling becomes your calling. As "one flesh" (Genesis 2:24), you identify with him in the mammoth responsibilities of the ministry. In fact, the success or failure of the young preacher just may rest in the influence of his mate.

Pray For Him Daily
That sounds trite, doesn't it? But here lies some of the power of the young preacher. Pray for him daily when you have your personal devotions. Write his name first in your prayer journal. Scribble his name in the flyleaf of your Bible to remind you to pray for him. Petition the Lord for special power and wisdom to rest upon your husband/pastor.

Tell Him You Are Praying
As you leave the auto, just before walking into the church building, say, "Honey, I'm praying for you today." When he leaves the home for the study, remind him that you are praying for him. Place a note in his Bible promising your prayer support. Give a note to an usher to take to your husband just before he preaches declaring your prayer support.

Take Notes While He Is Preaching

You may hear the same illustrations, outlines, and personal applications over and over again. But, by all means give your husband your undivided attention. Don't take your eyes off of him, unless you develop a habit of taking notes when he preaches.

In a notebook about the size of your Bible, record the date, place, text, and outline of his sermons. This will keep your mind occupied. Even as you take notes, still give your husband/pastor your attention. Many of those in the congregation go to sleep, talk, smack chewing gum, clip their fingernails, walk in and out, look at their watch, and pay very little attention to the man in the pulpit. The wife should not be guilty of anything that would rob the preacher/husband of preaching in spiritual power. Try to be engulfed in his message. Ask the Lord to speak to you from God's Word as your pastor and husband ministers from the pulpit.

Listen To The Young Preacher Vent His Feelings

The only person in the congregation who does not have a pastor is the pastor. Often the wife becomes a sounding board. Not an easy job! But, the young preacher needs someone to talk to, express his disappointments or encouragements, and share his burdens. It would be best to listen without comment. Refrain from spewing out comments that would stifle your husband's feelings. Be careful about harboring bad attitudes toward those in the congregation who cause your husband/pastor to "cry on your shoulder." Just listen! Try to be calm and not jump to conclusions. Remember that the man talking to you just may not have anyone else to share his burden, problems, and vision.

Refrain From Gossip

That which the preacher/husband tells his wife should be kept private. Never should the young preacher's wife tell other church members what he has shared in confidence. The best friend a young preacher should have should be his wife. She must listen without telling. She must remember that anything she tells a church member, even a family member, may be passed on to others, blown out of proportion, and gotten back to the wrong person. A gossiping young preacher's wife can destroy her husband's ministry. The wife must learn to be a deliverer of good news and squelch the bad.

Love Your Husband

Write him love notes. When he goes to preach in another church, put a note in one of his socks saying, "Sock it to them, Honey. I love you." Place a note in his shirt pocket stating, "My heart is next to your heart. I love you, Dear." Occasionally tape a note on the bathroom mirror expressing your love for him. The young preacher needs this encouragement from the one who understands him better than anyone else.

Be Faithful

In an age of infidelity, always be true to your preacher/husband. Treat him like a king. Never give him one ounce of suspicion about your loyalty to the marital vows. Set the example in the church congregation of devotion to your husband. Hold his hand in public. Treat him with utmost respect. Sit close to him in the church pew when another preacher is preaching. Stand at the

door with him when he shakes hands, unless small children demand otherwise. (Maybe the children could stand with you two at the front door.) Meet your husband's needs. The young preacher who finds love, peace, and happiness in his home will be able to better conduct a public ministry among many who don't have those blessings in their home.

Enjoy The Ministry

Pray for the ability to be an effective preacher's wife. Underline the instructions in Proverbs on how to accomplish this. Read books, listen to tapes, watch videos, and attend seminars that may equip you to more successfully serve with your mate. Major on enhancing his ministry. Take the back seat. Promote him. Serve hand-in-hand with your husband. And, reap the many wonderful rewards of ministering with the man of God in the ministry of proclaiming and practicing the Word of God.

The Challenge Of Being The Young Preacher's Mate

Proverbs declares, "A virtuous woman is a crown to her husband" and "Whoso findeth a wife findeth a good thing, and obtaineth favor of the Lord." A good wife is the most important ingredient to a good ministry. A young preacher's calling will be greatly affected by his wife. She will either be a blessing or a curse.

Permit me to speak to the wife of the young preacher. Young lady, you are becoming accustomed to living in the glass house of the church, often called a parsonage. Quite a challenge! But, also being a vital part of your husband's ministry can be a daily blessing that produces eternal rewards. Here are a few suggestions.

Be Quiet
Talking too much to church members can be detrimental to your husband's successful ministry. Remember that almost everything (if not everything) you say is going to be repeated. People just love to hear something, especially if it is bad, and tell someone else. Church members will lose respect for the pastor if his wife relates personal matters that should be kept in the prayer closet. That which transpires in the parsonage

should be kept in the parsonage. Furthermore, the wife must be extremely careful how she speaks about other church members. A good rule would be to only declare about others that which is good.

Be Submissive
Practice Ephesians 5 and submit to your preacher-husband. He should love you as the queen. You should love and respect him as the king. Church members are watching. The manner in which the young preacher and his wife treat each other publicly goes a long way in influencing other young couples.

Be Prayerful
The preacher-husband desperately needs a prayer warrior to soak him in prayer. While he is preparing sermons, pray for him. When he is visiting, call his name before the Lord. As he preaches, petition the Lord for His power to rest upon the one you love. Tell him as you walk into the church door, "Honey, I'm praying for you today." Write short notes, assuring him of your prayer support. Very few will pray for the man of God. His wife should.

Be Supportive
When the young preacher faces the firing squad of a deacon board, listen to your husband vent his feelings (without comment). Yes, he will make mistakes. But, don't rebuke him. That's the last thing he needs. When the situation calms down, then, and only then, ask him if you can discuss the matter and offer your suggestions or evaluation. The young preacher will be attacked. His wife is not called to organize a battalion and declare war upon the accusers. Better to pray for him. Assure your loved one with kind words of your support.

Quietly undergird your pastor-preacher-husband with the utmost support.

Be Faithful

Male church members or men at the office where you work may come at you with a vicious intent. Don't give them the time of the day. Yes, be friendly, smile, dress neatly and modestly. Never, never, leave the door cracked for a sexual advance. Men will repress their intentions if the woman will keep herself holy and free of intimate settings. Brag on your preacher-husband. Be by his side as much as possible. Kindly introduce your mate to every man you work with. Always give the impression you are happily married, committed to the Lord, satisfied with the church, and deeply in love with the man of your life.

Be Effective

The Lord anoints the young preacher's wife with special spiritual gifts, talents, and abilities. She should not spread herself too thin, but, by all means, devote her time to that which she does well. Participate in the activities of the church. Set the example. Being a younger person, the wife of the young preacher often will spend more time with the teens and children. That's good. But don't neglect the older ones in the congregation. A smiling, hand-shaking young pastor's wife, sharing kind words, will go a long way in assisting her husband minister effectively to the congregation.

The Children And Their Money

The goal of the parents is to produce children who practice stewardship, frugality, and selflessness.

Establish A Savings Account
In your child's name establish a savings account when he or she is born. Financial gifts to the child could be placed in that account rather than spend the money. If the bank will not allow savings accounts with a small deposit, purchase savings bonds or buy stock in the name of the child with you as the custodian.

Don't Buy A Lot Of Toys
Be selective at Christmas and birthdays. Two or three good gifts are better than numerous gifts, especially when grandparents and others buy gifts for the children. Teach the child to take care of the toys.

Establish A Financial Plan
The child needs to learn stewardship and frugality. Here is a good plan:

- Purchase a notebook and write each child's name in a divided section of the notebook.
- Make three sections under each child's name: Lord, savings, self. (10% for the Lord; 50% for personal savings; 40% for self)
- Give the child an allowance based on age.
- Teach the child to tithe on the allowance, money earned, and gifts.
- Deposit the 50% in a savings account or purchase savings bonds, designated for a Christian college education may be a good goal.
- Gifts given to the child would be his, unless he wanted to divide it according to the 10-50-40 schedule. Encourage the child to tithe on the gift.

It takes time to teach your child essential money principles. Most children can develop good habits of tithing, saving money, and knowing the value of personal finances if taught this method.

Teach Your Child The Value Of Money
Through practice and instruction teach the child to care for possessions, buy items on sale, wisely use money, and pray about purchases.

Buy Stock
Purchasing shares for the children, with you as the custodian, will increase your children's interest in the stock market. By using the reinvestment plan, the accounts will increase as the children grow older. The

dividends could be used for college education, purchases, wedding expenses, etc.

Financial Principles
Expect the child to help buy the car, assist in the purchase of clothes, and contribute in paying for college education. The parent is responsible to train the child in financial wisdom, rather than give him or her whatever is wanted.

What Is Learned Will Be Practiced
Children learn more by what is caught than taught. Tithing, exercising carefulness with money, saving -- all of these principles are learned as the children observe the practices of the parents.

"Train up a child in the way he should go," the Scriptures admonish parents. Financial training will benefit the child as he or she leaves home and sets up housekeeping. The parents should want to prepare the children for the real life — bills, responsibilities, saving, etc. All of this is accomplished when the boys and girls are growing up in the home.

Say "Thank You"

The young preacher, his wife, and family are often recipients of gifts and kind comments. These are usually expressions of love and appreciation. Learn to say "thank you" graciously.

A Thank-You Without Explanations
Maybe you did buy that pin-stripe suit at the second-hand store for just a few dollars. Possibly the widow did give you her deceased husband's suits. That pair of ten-year old shoes still shines with a gleam. Or, maybe you did purchase three shirts for the price of one. Great! All of this is wonderful. Praise the Lord!

Every kind comment does not demand an explanation. Don't tell anyone what you did or didn't pay for it. Just say "thank you." If members of your congregation are kind enough to state how nice you look in that blue suit with matching tie, you be just as kind by smiling and responding with a nod of gratitude.

If the one giving the compliment seems to want an answer, just reply that the Lord has been so good to provide your needs. Just learn to say "thank you!"

Write Thank-You Notes
Some church members enjoy expressing their appreciation for you and your ministry through gift-giving. A cake, a bag of tomatoes, a fifty-dollar bill, a birthday gift, a book for your library, a Christmas present — much appreciated gifts. All of the givers deserve a note of gratitude from you. If they are generous enough to share with you, you should be grateful enough to respond with a note of thanksgiving.

Purchase thank you notes by the box. Be sure to write a few words in the card, naming the gift. Express how much you appreciate the gift. Set a goal to mail the card within twenty-four hours.

Express Appreciation For Meals
The preacher is often blessed with meals provided in restaurants or homes during special church meetings, such as revival services and missionary conferences. Write a note of appreciation before going to bed that night. Mail the card the next day. If someone provides a dish of food, eat it all or empty the food into your own dish. Wash the bowl or plate. Place a note in the bottom of the dish, thanking the person for the delicious food. Return the dish immediately.

Practice Thanksgiving
Probably you could count your blessings all day. Living in an age of unthankfulness, the ambassador for Jesus Christ needs to intensify a spirit of gratitude. As a

young preacher, the Lord will use many different sources to meet your needs. Always display a grateful attitude. Most of God's creatures seem to take for granted His blessings. The young preacher should be the very opposite. Practice "thanksliving."

Write notes to your church members. Commend them for their faithfulness in Christian service. Assure those who are hurting of your prayer support. Express sincere gratitude to someone every day. A good time to do this would be on their birthday.

Be A Grateful Husband
The wife cooks the meals, cleans the home, rears the children, answers the telephone, smiles when she doesn't feel like smiling, and attends all of the church services. She may wait with you until the last person leaves the church services. She deserves notes of thanksgiving from the lips and actions of her preacher husband. Too often the young preacher takes his dear wife for granted. He may congratulate, commend, praise, and exalt almost everyone in the congregation and forget the one who means the most to him. Learn to practice thanksgiving first at home.

Count Your Blessings
All of us enjoy being around someone who is thankful and excited about God's abundant blessings. The young preacher needs to learn early in his ministry how to practice thanksgiving in the pulpit, parsonage, and public life. It is contagious!

SEE THE FORM FOR RECORDING THE GIFTS

GIFTS FROM CHURCH MEMBERS

DATE   GIFT GIVEN   DATE OF RESPONSE

_____
_____
_____
_____
_____
_____
_____
_____
_____
_____
_____
_____
_____
_____
_____
_____
_____
_____
_____
_____
_____
_____

PERSONAL FINANCES

PLANS FOR THE NEW YEAR

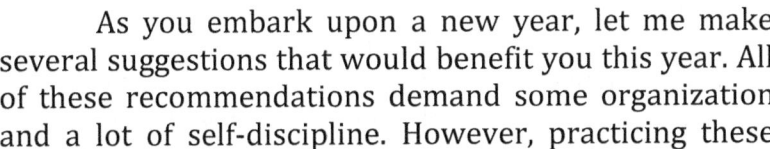

As you embark upon a new year, let me make several suggestions that would benefit you this year. All of these recommendations demand some organization and a lot of self-discipline. However, practicing these suggestions will produce much profit and personal satisfaction.

Save All Sale Receipts
Designate a box for you, your wife, and the entire family to deposit all receipts from every purchase. A long wooden or metal recipe box would be ideal. Place the container in the kitchen or a place that is easily accessible. Remind all of the family members (kindly, of course) throughout the year to place the receipts in the box. You'll be surprised at how many times you will dig through that special box searching for a receipt of an item you want to return. Often merchandise will break or prove to be of inferior quality. The receipt will assist you in returning the item to secure a replacement without additional charge.

At the end of the year, place all of the receipts in a file folder and label it _ RECEIPTS (the year). Then, next January start all over again and place all of the receipts in the same box. Each year file the receipts. You'll also be surprised at how you will refer back to a file two or three years old to retrieve a sales receipt to prove that you purchased a certain item at a certain price.

Place All Warranties In A File

Most purchases carry a warranty. Even a small watch, a water hose, a tool, etc., provide some type of warranty. That new purchase may appear to be unbreakable. Don't assume that. The average shopper will find at least one or two items every year that break or do not work efficiently. Warranties or guarantees should be placed in a file. Every couple of years you could thumb through the file and destroy the warranties that are out of date.

Get A Will

I was "afraid" to go the lawyer's office and secure a legal will. In the back of my mind something seemed to tell me that registering a will would mean that I would die soon after. My brother-in-law died at age 38, leaving behind a wife and four children. I immediately went to the lawyer's office and had a will drawn up for my wife, the children, and myself.

You don't want the courts to determine who takes care of your children if you and the mate die at the same time. Get a will! Do it today!

Plan A Budget

With pencil and paper or a computer program, record all of your expected expenses for the upcoming year. Try to account for all of the anticipated income. Then, balance the two. Included in the budget should be the tithe to your church, offerings, taxes, auto expenses, home mortgage and/or housing expenses, medical bills, food, clothing, recreation, education, etc.

If the budget just won't balance, make the shortage a daily matter of prayer. As you exercise frugality, give to the Lord, and pray, you will be pleasantly surprised to watch the Lord send in additional funds. A simple budget will reveal where your money goes and how you need to cut out unnecessary expenses.

Develop A Financial File

During the year, place receipts of items that are tax deductible in designated files. For example, auto, housing, office, books, newspapers, magazines, medical bills, etc., can often be used to reduce your taxes. By placing the receipts during the year in the different files, your preparation for filing income taxes is much easier.

Set Some Spiritual Goals For The New Year

Determine where you will read in your Bible this upcoming year. I read the four gospels over and over again for three years in a row. I read Acts through Revelation several times one year. Then, this past year I very slowly read the history book of Acts. What a blessing! Just make up your mind the direction of your devotional Bible reading and stick with it day-by-day.

Write down in your prayer journal some spiritual goals for this year. For example, witness to an unsaved person every day, pass out a certain number of tracts each week, fast and pray during certain times, write a missionary each week, visit a mission field, write out a sermon each week, visit in a rest home each week, and many other goals you could personally make.

List Your Prayer Requests

Pray expecting God to answer! This year can be even more exciting as you check off your prayer requests as they are answered. List the names of hardened sinners. Write down the seemingly impossible prayer burdens. Record personal and family requests. This New Year may be the best you have ever experienced since becoming a Christian.

Expect A Great Year

Be optimistic. Stop grumbling. Approach every new day with enthusiasm. Express your love to the wife and children on a daily basis. Stop looking in; look out to help meet the needs of others. Live every day as if that day the Lord may return. Young preacher, it is going to be a good year as the Lord ministers to our every need for His own honor and glory. Don't miss the blessings!

SET GOALS

Setting personal goals is essential for accomplishing anything worthwhile. Goals give a sense of direction and purpose, promote daily enthusiasm, facilitate effective operation, reduce wasting time, and accomplish far more than would be achieved without goals. Goals act as a measuring stick to determine what we are accomplishing. Without goals we have activity but often little productivity. Just being busy is not necessarily rewarding at the end of the day.

Weekly Goals

On Sunday evening or Monday morning, make a list of everyone you want to call by telephone during the week. List those you want to visit. Record the names of those you want to write. Write down in your planner the sermons you must preach, the items for the bulletin, and the church responsibilities. Record EVERYTHING in that planner that must be accomplished. MARK EACH ITEM OFF AS IT IS DONE. This will give you a sense of accomplishment and reveal what still must be done. If a goal is not achieved, shift it to the next day or week. Be determined to check it off just as soon as possible.

Yearly Goals

Include in this list the sermon plans. For example, you may want to preach through a certain book of the Bible on Sunday morning, another book or topic on Sunday evening, and yet another subject matter on Wednesday evening. By determining the direction of your preaching you will spend far less time "looking for sermons" and far more time in preparation. And, just because you have set preaching goals does not mean that you can't deviate a Sunday or two and preach on another subject.

Also, good yearly goals include listing the books you want to read, a Bible reading schedule, the article you want to write for a magazine, a vacation you want to enjoy, etc. Financial goals are good -- the amount of the tithe and the schedule for placing money in a savings account.

Physical goals are excellent, such as the weight that needs to be lost or gained, the lowering or raising of the cholesterol - all of these, plus more, should be written down at the beginning of the year. Set goals and accomplish more!

Five-Year Goals

Setting goals for the church is valuable for the productive pastor. Record those goals in your prayer book. Do not reveal them to the congregation. Pray. Work toward achieving those goals. Set monetary goals, such as new pews, a paved parking lot, a parsonage or housing allowance, landscaping of the church grounds, etc. Pray daily for five years and watch the Lord meet these needs during those sixty months. Spiritual goals are appropriate, too. Record in your prayer book the names of those you want to make decisions for Christ. Beside church members' names, state a goal, such as "overcoming a temper," "stop smoking," "become a soul winner," "be willing to teach a Sunday School class." Put a check and a date beside the names of those who achieve spiritual growth. Again, do not share with the congregation your goals.

Life Goals

Where do you want to be spiritually by age thirty? How many times do you want to read the Bible through? How many verses do you want to memorize? How much daily time do you want to spend in prayer? Visit a mission field? Write a book? Outline the entire Bible? Hundreds of goals are out there, young preacher. Be sure to write down these goals in your planning book or prayer journal. The faith-plans will be a daily reminder. And, you will never hit any of them unless you aim.

End-Of-Life Goals

How much do you want to have in investments by retire age? Social Security just may not provide an adequate life style. The best time to begin working on goals for the sunset years is now — today, young preacher! Saving five dollars a week is better than nothing. Making even small contributions regularly to the Board of Retirement will be far more productive at the end of your ministry than if you neglect to participate in this excellent plan.

Goals Are Personal

No one will set the goals for us. The young preacher probably will not be accountable to anyone for his goal-setting and goal-achieving. All of this is a personal matter. Goals demand prayer. "Lord, what do you want me to do today? Tomorrow? This year? The next few years?" Surely the Lord has specific and productive plans for our lives. Discover His will. Make a plan." Aim toward the mark for the prize ..." You'll be glad you did.

PAY FOR A CAR

One of the pastor's largest expenses is his automobile. He must have one. The church members expect it to look new. It must be large enough to accommodate his family and take others to church services.

The car must be in good condition, ready to make a hospital trip late at night or lead a funeral procession. The pastor's car is an expensive necessity, and often his car allowance doesn't cover the expenses. How can the young pastor spend less on the automobile? Here are some suggestions:

Select A Used Car.
Purchasing a new car is too expensive. Choose one that will handle the size of your family today and three years from now. Resist the temptation to purchase a new car. Don't even look at them.

Pay For The Car.

As soon as possible, payoff the lending institution. Debt may be necessary for the first car, but eliminate that debt quickly.

Establish A Car Fund.

Once the present car is paid for, establish a savings account. Have the bank draft your checking account a certain amount each month (preferably what you were paying on the previous car debt) to be transferred into your car fund. When that fund accumulates to about $500, invest the money in a higher yield account. Don't touch the money. It's better to take out a bank loan for emergencies rather than deplete your car fund.

Set A Mileage Goal.

Plan to drive your present car 100,000 miles. Once that's accomplished, you will delight in driving the auto toward another 100,000 miles.

Don't Trade On Impulse Or Aggravation. Repair the car if at all possible. Yes, it may cost. But compare the repair cost to a bank note for a newer car. You can pay for a lot of repairs cheaper than buying a new car.

Keep The Car Serviced.

A busy preacher is too busy if he can't wash and vacuum his car at least twice a month. Get it serviced regularly. Remember, the better the old auto looks the more valuable it is when you want to sell it later.

Finally, Time To Buy A Newer Car.

The old car is about dead. Plan ahead. Read the newspaper ads daily for several weeks. Ask the Lord to lead you to the best buy. Don't get in a hurry.

Set A Goal To Drive A Quality Auto That Is Paid For.

It may take you several years but it can be accomplished. A more expensive, heavier car may cost more initially, yet be less expensive to operate over a period of years. Don't let members intimidate you when you drive a car that looks expensive. At least it is paid for!

READ THREE BOOKS AT A TIME

"Apply thine heart unto instruction; and thine ears to the words of knowledge"
(Proverbs 23:12).

The busy preacher must read his Bible, the most important book in his possession. He must read it, meditate upon it, preach it, and live it.

But other reading is profitable also. The young preacher should read at least three books at one time. Here are some suggestions.

Keep A Book In Your Car.
Probably light, easy reading — a biography or how-to-do-it book. Or maybe a devotional book. While traveling or visiting you may be delayed by a draw bridge, traffic jam or auto break-down. You may arrive at the bank too early. Don't waste time. Be prepared with a challenging book. "Redeem the time."

Read A Second Book At Home.
Read in the bedroom, bathroom, or den. Try to read a chapter a day.

Place The Third Book In Your Study.
After studying or counseling, stand up and read a chapter in that book. Walk around the office and read.

By reading three books simultaneously, you'll surprise yourself by how many books you read in a year. Keep a list of the books you read in a notebook.

Always keep a stack of books on your "wait list." As you finish one of your three books, replace it with another. Do not hesitate to read some books twice. A. W. Tozer's books can be read over and over again.

Shop second-hand book stores. Borrow books from the library or another pastor friend. Swap books. Set a goal to read a certain number of books each year. You'll be pleased by how much simultaneous reading expands your ministry. And you can accomplish this in only a few minutes each day.

SHOULD A YOUNG PREACHER HAVE A WILL?

A will is a legal document. The written record expresses a person's personal desires and plans for earthly possessions. The average young preacher declares, "I don't have enough to get a will!" Or, he states, "I'm afraid to get a will. I may die the next day." That was my opinion until my brother-in-law died at age thirty-eight in a single vehicle accident. As soon as my wife and I got back home, we immediately began to prepare our financial affairs in case of our deaths.

One of those things that I had put off was drawing up a will, which we did soon in an attorney's office. Death did not claim our lives the day after we signed the papers, but my wife and I did have a greater peace of mind. Especially did we feel better about our five children's living conditions if both of us died at the same time.

The Necessity Of A Will
Young preacher, you may possess more than you realize. Maybe two vehicles, a home, a life insurance policy or two, an inheritance, furniture, savings, investments — it adds up. A will declares that the living spouse will receive all of the possessions of the deceased spouse without any legal difficulties. Surely the young preacher wants to be assured of this guarantee.

The Wisdom Of A Will

Every young couple with young children should have a will to provide for the care of the children in the event both parents die at the same time. Or, possibly one parent dies in an automobile accident and the other parent is in a coma in the hospital. A properly written will guarantees the placement of the children in a home where the couple selects, not the court system. In our first will, my wife and I stated that we wanted all five of our children to be placed in the same Children's Home so they would not be separated. Thankfully that never became necessary, but it could have happened.

The Executor Of The Will

In the event of the death of both parents simultaneously, it is wise to declare an executor in the will. The executor will be responsible to file all of the necessary forms, pay all expenses, and make proper distributions. Maybe a bank officer, or a trusted friend, or a child could serve in this capacity. The young preacher may think he is going to live almost to one-hundred, but he may not. It is better to plan as if an executor will be needed.

The Provisions In A Will

If the young preacher wants to leave ten per cent to his church after his estate is settled, the will would be an ideal document to assure this plan. If personal possessions with sentimental value need to be passed on to certain children, the will could accomplish this. Certain statements could be made. For example, Patrick Henry declared the testimony of his conversion in his will, I understand.

The Legality Of A Will

Should a computer program be purchased? Can one write his own will? It is possible to draft a will without an attorney, but there is a tremendous risk in doing so. I would recommend spending a few dollars for a peace of mind. Also, if a move to another state becomes necessary, it may be wise to determine if it is required by law to update the will. Considering the importance of this document, it is most important that every aspect of the will be completely legal and executable.

The Greatest Problem

Procrastination. Very few people die while sitting in an attorney's office signing a will. The young preacher needs to deal with this fear. Make an appointment today with the legal advisor. When an estate is in order, an emotional load disappears. Besides, a family may be saved from regret and hardship.

TAXES

The young preacher must learn early in the ministry how to satisfy the Internal Revenue Service. Specific rules apply to ministers and churches. Both should be very careful to abide by the rules for testimony sake and for obedience to the law.

When the pastor understands the financial aspects of the ministry, he can reduce the risk of an IRS audit. I recommend purchasing the Ministers Tax Guide from Worth Tax and Financial Service. Follow that guide exactly as presented. B.J. Worth also conducts seminars in several states each year.

File Income Taxes Properly
The minister must establish proper procedures for filing his taxes. First, the pastor is considered by the Internal Revenue Service to be an employee of the church. The church treasurer is expected to provide the pastor with a Form W-2 at the end of each year of just the actual salary. Housing and auto allowances and most other allowances should not be included in this form. If the minister does not spend all of one or more of those allowances, he should report that as income in his personal income tax reporting.

The minister must report his salary in the quarterly Form 941. Also, the minister is responsible to pay the FICA taxes. This should be calculated on the Schedule SE and pay this tax when the Form 1040 is filed.

Church Withhold Taxes

The church treasurer or bookkeeper may withhold a sufficient amount from the pastor's salary to cover federal and state income taxes, plus enough for the self-employment taxes. These amounts withheld must be reported to the proper agencies and on time. A young preacher may hesitate discussing these matters with a church treasurer, especially if he or she is the only church employee. That is why it would be wise to purchase B.J. Worth's book every year, mark clearly the information that the church must do, and then share it with the treasurer or bookkeeper. The records are not as complicated as they may appear to a dedicated, volunteer church treasurer. The young preacher must explain the forms carefully and kindly.

Read The Financial Guidelines

The young preacher would profit greatly by reading the material on his financial responsibilities to the government. Contact the Internal Revenue Service for booklets. Visit the local library to read magazines and books on this subject.

Understand Clergy Compensation

Besides the salary provided by the church, I trust that your pastorate provides other benefits, such as medical insurance, auto allowance, housing provision, and ministry allowances. An accountable expense reimbursement plan would provide documented expenses. If documented correctly, reimbursed expenses do not have to be reported for tax purposes. The preacher absolutely should write down auto expenses, hospitality costs, and depreciation on personally-owned office equipment, subscriptions, books, long-distance phone calls for the church or ministry, etc. The IRS provides reasonable methods for these expenses to be documented that the young preacher should follow.

My Salary Is Small!

Yes, most ministers do not receive adequate pay. Nor are they reimbursed for the time and energy expended on behalf of the church. That is why the young preacher and his family must stretch every dollar as far as possible. A workable budget, a satisfactory bookkeeping system, and an adequate plan of paying taxes are essential. I challenge you to start today. April 15 appears on the calendar quicker than you anticipate.

TRY TO LEAD YOUR CHURCH FINANCIALLY

Most young preachers pastor smaller churches. Often the financial policies are already established. The philosophy "we have always done it that way" has prevailed many years. And, the young preacher will be unwise to attempt many changes at first. He must gain the respect and trust of the congregation. That may take several years.

The young preacher should set some goals for the congregation that God has allowed him to pastor. He should at least try to prepare the way for the next pastor.

Prepare A Budget
Leading the deacons or a finance committee to prepare a budget may be the first step to give directions to the church finances. I had rather call it a "faith financial guide." The first budgets should be short, maybe including the main essentials, such as pastor's provisions, church operation, and outreach ministries. Encourage the church leaders to re-evaluate the financial guide annually. If the church has not used a budget, it may take you several years to lead the congregation in this endeavor.

As the church accepts the advantages of the budget, you may feel free to make suggestions that certain pastoral provisions be added. For example, the pastor's travel allowance, medical insurance, social security, retirement, church meetings, and housing could be added to the budget.

A good method of determining the pastor's financial provisions would be to ask the deacons, church board, or finance committee who are actively working to write down their total salary. Then get the average salary among those men. That average would be a good norm for the pastor's total provisions. (It would be much better if one of the church leaders would conduct this poll and ask the men to submit their salary package anonymously.)

Auto Allowance

One of the most expensive responsibilities for the pastor is sustaining an adequate vehicle. The busy pastor may drive from 20,000 to 30,000 miles a year. Most of that mileage occurs when he travels to the hospitals, visiting, participating in church meetings, and traveling to and from the church facilities. A good method of providing the pastor's auto allowance is to determine what the government allows for income tax purposes. Multiply that by the average number of miles the pastor drives annually transacting church business.

Medical Insurance

Providing medical coverage for the pastor and his family benefits the church as well as the pastor. A caring church would want to provide for the pastor and his family in the event of illness. That would be better accomplished through providing adequate medical coverage. Better to pay monthly premiums than for the church feel obligated to take up large, special offerings to help the pastor pay off medical bills. Often group policies are available at a discount rate for the young pastor.

Retirement Benefit

Help yourself, as well as the next pastor, by establishing a retirement program in the church budget. If you leave the church, this important provision would probably be continued for the next young pastor. A monthly contribution to a pension plan would grow quickly and painlessly if it is included in the church budget. This forced retirement plan would help the young preacher prepare for a future that he may not consider now. Retirement age will arrive much faster than expected.

Social Security

Some churches pay at least half of the pastor's social security. Many pay all of it. Very few churches could continue to pay the salary of a disabled pastor while employing a new pastor. It could be to the benefit of the church to pay the social security premium.

Church Representation

The pastor represents the church in the district, state, and national meetings. The budget should include adequate reimbursement for mileage, food, and housing.

Parsonage Or Housing Allowance?

Many churches are discussing the advantages and disadvantages of owning a parsonage. Quite a few churches are providing an adequate housing allowance to cover the mortgage, insurance, taxes, utilities, and upkeep for their pastor's own home. Usually a housing allowance allows the pastor to build up equity in a home. The young preacher who settles in for the long haul may prove to the church the advantages of their providing him a housing allowance. This relieves the church of the responsibility of providing the upkeep for a parsonage.

Exercise Patience

It may take many years to establish a workable faith financial guide. With increased costs, the guide will probably need to be changed every year. The young preacher must exercise much patience and wisdom as he leads his congregation in financial matters. You must not think of only yourself. You may not pastor that particular group of people the entire ministry. Therefore, whatever financial suggestions you make to the board or church, you should keep in mind the needs of the pastor who follows you.

YOUR LIBRARY

"Take fast hold of instruction; let her not go"
(Proverbs 4:13).

A preacher without books is like a plumber without a wrench, a fisherman with no net or a carpenter with no hammer.

The preacher has no shortcut to an effective pulpit ministry; he must have tools. To construct a sermon, the preacher needs a Bible, commentary, Bible dictionary, concordance, and other helps. He approaches the building and preserving of his library as precisely as a contractor prepares to erect a house.

The preacher's books are an investment. Just as a mechanic protects his valuable tool box so the preacher preserves his tools of paper.

Plan Your Library
Don't buy everything that looks good. Set priorities. Get the basic needs and then build on that. Ask older ministers for a suggested list.

Buy Books
Buy at least one book a month. If you must skip a meal or two, buy books regularly.

Look For Books
Be alert at yard sales, flea markets, and store sales for books that will enhance your library.

Take An Inventory
Someone in your church may be willing to do this for you. Make three copies of your book list. File those copies in different places: home and church.

Place Your Books On Shelves In Categories
Categorize your books such as biographies, Christian living, church history, New Testament, Old Testament, etc.

Insure Your Books
Many preachers have lost their libraries when the church caught on fire. Possibly the church insurance does not cover your own personal library.

Take A Picture Of Your Library
Secure tangible proof of your library with photos or videos. Place the photos or videos at another location.

Use The Books
Tools left on a shelf are of no value. Refer to the books regularly. If you loan them, place a sheet of paper at the end of the book shelf and record the date, person who borrowed the book, and the name of the book.

Include In Your Will
Your will should include the exact distribution of your books. Designate the college, pastor, or young preacher who you want to receive your library at your death.

Don't Worship Books
Appreciate their value, but be willing to keep the library in a box in the attic if the Lord moves you to a church where there is no room for a study.

The Most Important Book
The Bible is the most important book in your library. It is good to read as many books as possible, but daily absorb your soul and mind in the Word of God.

HAVE A GARDEN

"He that tilletb his land shall be satisfied with bread"
(Proverbs 12:11).

Not too large. Most young preachers do not have the time for a garden any larger than 30" x 30". But from just a few tomato plants to several rows, the young preacher and his family will benefit from growing vegetables in his back yard.

Good Therapy. After preparing messages, visiting and handling church administration, it's refreshing to concentrate your attention on something that doesn't talk back but grows exactly where you put it. Sowing seed and watching God produce the fruit of your labors is exciting.

Good Exercise. A back yard garden demands walking, bending, pulling and perspiring. It doesn't cost as much as golf or bowling. In fact, this exercise is an investment that pays good dividends.

Profitable. Besides the delicious, nutritional vegetables, the gardener will save several hundreds of dollars in his food bill.

Opportunity For Witnessing. Neighbors talk more freely to a gardener. Across-the- fence witnessing can be most effective. Even sharing some of the fruit of the field softens the heart of an unsaved neighbor who has some reservations about the preacher next door.

A Blessing To Others. Sharing vegetables with older members of the congregation can be a personal blessing as well as providing some of their needs.

AND HOW? Renting or borrowing a tiller would be less expensive than buying one. Take a soil sample. Choose the best spot. Don't till too big a spot. Plan your rows. Buy and sow the seed. Put leaves around the plants for mulch to keep out grass. Enjoy the vegetables.

PRAY FOR MISSIONARIES

*"... the Lord heareth the prayer of the righteous.
The light of the eyes rejoiceth the heart:
and a good report makes the bones fat"
(Proverbs 15:29b-30).*

The pastor should pray for those who spread the gospel. Through praying for missionaries by name, the pastor gets personally involved in world-wide evangelization. Here's how a busy pastor can pray for missionaries and fields daily.

- Make a list of all the missionaries and fields you know.
- Divide that list into five equal parts. Type the list and place it in your Bible.
- Pray for the first section Monday, the second Tuesday, etc.
- Pray for missionary leaders and other pastors on Saturday and Sunday.
- When missionary prayer requests arrive, write them on your prayer sheet.
- Write or e-mail the missionaries at least once a year. Tell them you pray for them. A good time to write is on their birthdays.

- Share missionary information with the congregation and pray publicly for the requests.
- Invite missionaries to your home or study. Record their prayer requests. Pray with them.
- Personally support missionaries through the faith-promise plan.
- Encourage your congregation to pray for missionaries by name.
- Include missionary prayer requests in the church bulletin.
- Encourage church members to write missionaries. During the mid-week service ask them to share prayer requests from missionaries.
- Preach on prayer and the emphasis that the Apostle Paul gave to praying for missionaries.

HOW TO MAKE YOUR CLOTHES LAST LONGER

Ants are not strong; neither are preachers rich. But ants prepare for the winter, and preachers must be just as wise in providing adequate clothing in a profession that demands clean, neat, durable apparel on a limited income.

Purchase quality clothes at sale prices. Special purchases or some sale items may not be the best deal. Check local stores for the regular price of clothes you want to wear. Then wait for the merchandise to go on sale.

- Rotate wearing your clothes. Hang them in a closet with plenty of space.

- Do not hang your clothes on bedposts, doorknobs, or chairs.

- When you come home, change clothes immediately unless you plan to leave again in a few hours. Hang the good clothes in the closet and put on neat, casual clothes.

- Have your clothes cleaned periodically. Even though it's expensive, you extend the life of the apparel.

- Examine your ties regularly for food spots. Discard, wash or get cleaned.

- Polish your shoes weekly. Keep a shine rag in your study and car for quick brush ups.

- Install plastic taps to avoid wearing out shoe heels.

- For good stewardship, wear your clothes and shoes as long as possible.

- Purchase the same style and color of socks. Connect your socks together immediately when you take them off so they will not get lost in the washing machine. (You can buy small, round, plastic connectors that work well.)

- Purchase clothes that match and can be used interchangeably.

- Remove stains immediately. Talcum powder works wonders.

Don't be ashamed to wear an apron in the kitchen or place a napkin in your lap at the table.

A good dresser doesn't have to be rich, just wise and frugal.

THE YOUNG PREACHER'S HEALTH

*"And thou mourn at the last; when thy flesh
and thy body are consumed"
(Proverbs 5:11).*

The young preacher has energy to burn. He often acts as if he thinks he will never get sick or die. He considers it his responsibility to burn the candle at both ends. But the scriptures command us to take care of our bodies. The young preacher is wise to consider some suggestions that may lengthen his ministry and cause him to be more fruitful:

- Get seven to eight hours of sleep each night.
- Eat breakfast.
- Eat nutritional meals.
- Try to eat as little as possible after 5:00 p.m.
- Take a bath daily; wash your hair regularly.
- Wash your hands after each hospital visit.
- Gargle with a strong mouthwash before leaving home or the study (for the benefit of others).

- Gargle for your benefit when you return.
- Take vitamins daily.
- Floss your teeth daily.
- Brush your teeth after every meal.
- Clean your nails regularly. Don't bite your nails.
- Walk the steps at the hospital rather than ride the elevator.
- Drink juices daily.
- Drink several glasses of water daily.
- Eat honey regularly, preferably from the area where you live. (Honey contains vitamins, promotes sound sleep, and keeps down allergies.)
- Exercise daily. Walk at least one mile, ride an exercise bike, or do exercises in the home or study.
- Train yourself to breathe deeply.
- Have a garden, cut the grass, rake the leaves, shovel the snow. Eat some fruit daily.
- Sit and stand straight.

PRACTICE FRUGALITY

Most young preachers do not earn a very large salary. In fact, the challenge facing the majority of young men in a smaller church will be to keep his head above the financial waters. Just to pay the bills, and maybe save a little for the future, will demand great skill. The young preacher and his family will need to exercise some principles of financial survival.

Be Content
Paul the Apostle declared, "Not that I speak in respect of want: for I have learned, in whatsoever state I am, therewith to be content." The preacher must learn early in the ministry to refrain from "keeping up with the." Some of your church members will throw away more on pet projects than you will ever earn. Also, be glad they can buy a new vehicle every year or two. Rejoice with them when they build a new home. Express thanksgiving unto the Lord when they get promotions that produce better salaries. But, don't get jealous! The Lord has called you to minister His Word, maybe live in a house the church owns, and possibly wonder at times how you are going to buy groceries. Grumbling or developing a sour spirit will not accomplish a single

thing. But, watching God meet your daily needs will deepen your faith and strengthen you for future challenges.

May I encourage you to tithe faithfully on all the Lord sends your way, exercise frugality (some called it stinginess), and trust the Lord to miraculously meet your every need.

Be Careful
The funds the Lord blesses you with will go farther if you exercise financial self-discipline. To stretch every dollar just as far as it will extend should be your daily commitment. Let me make some suggestions.

- Refrain from buying merchandise unless it is sold at a reduced price. Shop the end of the season sales.

- Payoff credit card purchases every month. Refuse to be under the control of a piece of plastic.

- Be determined to drive a vehicle just as many miles as possible. Keep it clean. Service it regularly. Pay off the debt and begin to save for the next auto.

- Be practical in saving money, such as turn off the water when you brush your teeth, switch off lights when you leave the room, change and hang up your clothes when you come home from church services, tear napkins or paper towels in half, write post cards instead of letters, whenever possible. Don't join book or music clubs. Shut the refrigerator door quickly and completely. Control the thermostat carefully and sleep in a cool room. Plan trips to eliminate driving extra miles, etc

Be Cautious

Pay your bills as quickly as possible. Set a goal to live "debt free." The only possible large debts may be a vehicle and a home. But, be determined to payoff both of these ahead of schedule. Debt should not hinder a preacher from doing God's will. Often the young preacher will be so burdened with bills that he just cannot function properly as a minister.

Be Conscientious

Plan ahead. The young preacher must ask himself, "How would my wife pay the bills in the event of my sickness, disability, or death?" A long, hard look must be given to certain possibilities that would deplete the young preacher living in a parsonage with very few savings and an insufficient income. Much prayer and study must be exercised to determine how you would provide for the family if tragedy struck. There are some preparations that must be carefully considered, such as insurance, savings, investments, etc.

Be Considerate

Consider your own body. As stewards, we are responsible to take care of the body. No one else will do it for you. Preventative maintenance can save money, lots of money. By getting the teeth cleaned twice a year, keeping the blood pressure and blood sugar under control, exercising regularly, eating well balanced meals, refusing to eat many sweets, drinking plenty of water, sleeping seven to eight hours each night — this, plus more, will assist in saving money in the long run. Just eliminating a visit to the doctor or the hospital will surely save bundles.

Be Committed

How much debt do you want next year? How much do you want in savings in five years? Where do you want to be financially when age 65 is reached? The young preacher has far more opportunities for investing that the older preacher ever thought possible. Age 60 or 65 may seem a long way down the road. Young preacher, it is much shorter than you could ever imagine. Preparation must be made now, not later.

Be Confident

Yes, trust the Lord. He knows your every need. However, remember that you are classified "self-employed." Most churches are not in position, or either they do not elect, to establish you on a firm, financial footing. You must do it yourself. Give it some thought, brother. Seek some counsel. Get a plan. Stick to the plan the rest of your life. Be willing to make some financial sacrifices. You'll be glad you did!

PREPARING FOR THE FUTURE

Possibly you signed the waiver to be exempt from contributing to the Social Security system. I will not discuss in this article the pros and cons of your decision. However, please give me your undivided attention if you write "Exempt Form 4361" on your tax return each year. Your decision declares that you are conscientiously opposed to the acceptance of public insurance and medical benefits. Therefore, you are not required by law to deduct 15.3% from your salary provision to the Internal Revenue Service.

Have You Considered The Future?
I personally believe that the young preacher should invest wisely the amount that he does not pay into the Social Security program. Too many older preachers have neglected to exercise this wise stewardship. The ministry has rushed by. Retirement or disability, without adequate provisions, are facing many men of God who have burned out their lives in the ministry. The young preacher must begin now. Waiting another day is too late.

Wise Stewardship

"I can't afford it!" You cannot afford not to, Brother! Would your widow have the finances to bury you this week in the event of your death? ("Oh, young preachers don't die," you say. Write or e-mail me. I can give you the names of several preachers who have died in their thirties.) Would your widow have enough funds to help her get settled in another town? Is money available to send the children to college? "The church will provide financial assistance," you declare. Now, brother, think that statement through. Most churches are not going to sustain a new pastor financially plus support your family. If you don't exercise wise stewardship, no one is going to do it for you.

Begin A Program

There are many avenues for you to follow. Let me make a few suggestions. (Some other ministers may advise you differently.) But, develop your own plan. Stick to it. Procrastination is not only the trap door over the pit of hell. But, putting off responsibilities also plagues many preachers.

First, bank free. Visit several banks and determine how this can be accomplished. Refuse to pay service charges. Second, establish a savings account. Let the bank transfer from your checking account a certain amount each month to the savings account. Don't touch that savings account! If you must borrow money, possibly you may want to use that account as collateral (borrow from yourself) and pay it back as quickly as possible. Third, establish a tax sheltered plan or an Individual Retirement Account (IRA).

Insurance?

For the young preacher, term insurance until about age fifty would be the least expensive. How much? Determine the funds your widow would need to get settled in a home if you are living in a parsonage. Leave her enough provisions for five years of financial security. Consider the number of children the Lord has blessed you with and determine how much they will need for a Christian college education.

Medical Insurance?

Medical coverage should be provided by the church you pastor. Such an adequate provision would greatly benefit the church, especially in the event of a serious illness by the pastor or one of the family members. Shop around. Seek group coverage, if at all possible. You may want to evaluate some of the Christian organizations that provide medical benefits.

Where Do I Get The Money?

The 15.3%. If you are not paying that amount to the Social Security system, I believe you are obligated to take that exact figure and invest it wisely for the benefit of your family. Determine the amount 15.3% represents. Sixty-dollars a week? One-hundred dollars a week? Write it on a piece of paper. From that figure, begin to place so much in a savings account, an IRA, insurance protection, annuities, mutual funds, etc. Discipline yourself. Young preachers have far greater opportunities today to make wise investments than older ministers had when they were your age.

What If You Pay Into Social Security?

The Social Security provision at age 62 or 65 or more will not adequately fund you with a lifestyle that you are presently enjoying. The program was not established to do so. The wise, young preacher should project his mind thirty or forty years ahead. Where do you want to be financially at retirement? Divide that number by the number of years before you reach 62. Then, establish a financial plan to systematically set aside so many dollars each week to reach that goal. "The Lord will return before I reach retirement!" you piously declare. When I was a student at Bob Jones University in the late 50's that is the reason several students gave for dropping out of college and beginning their ministry. On the day this article is being written, the Lord has not yet come, I have longed for His return every day. But, that excuse is not good enough to refrain from making wise investments for the possible "rainy days." So, brother, designate two hours this week, establish the 15.3% amount, and sharpen your pencil to determine the amount you must take out of your salary provision each week to invest for the protection of your family. I'll be with the Lord by the time you reach retirement. Either you or your widow just may place flowers on my grave in Ayden, North Carolina, and utter a prayer of thanksgiving for the above suggestions.

FINANCIAL PRINCIPLES FROM PROVERBS

Work

There are at least three ways to make money: work, steal, or receive an inheritance. Working is an honorable way. Proverbs 6:6-8 declares, "*Go to the ant, thou sluggard; consider her ways, and be wise: which having no guide, overseer, or ruler, provideth her meat in the summer, and gathereth her food in the harvest.*" You would benefit and the Lord would be glorified if the pastor were known for his hard work. And, what is work for the preacher? "But we will give ourselves continually to prayer and to the ministry of the word," the apostles told the disciples in Acts 6. Praying, preparing sermons, preaching should be the priority. Everything else should be secondary.

Avoid Debt

"*The rich ruleth over the poor, and the borrower is servant to the lender,*" Proverbs 22:7 states. You should shun debt, paying cash for everything possible. A vehicle and a home may be the exception, but even then it would be far better to eliminate those debts as quickly as possible.

Pay Your Bills When Due

Telephone, utility, vehicle expenses, clothes, food, etc. bills do appear regularly. Proverbs 3:27- 28 declares, *"Withhold not good from them to whom it is due, when it is in the power of thine hand to do it. Say not unto thy neighbor, go, and come again, and tomorrow I will give; when thou hast it by thee."* You will produce a poor testimony if bills are not paid when they come due. Better to do without than have and can't pay.

Avoid Money Making Schemes

Proverbs 13: 11 states, *"Wealth gotten by vanity (dishonesty) shall be diminished; but he that gathereth by labour shall increase."* Quite a few people will ask for an appointment to influence you to join them in money making ideas. Don't get caught up in these traps. Better to look to the Lord for financial solvency than the world's methods.

Spend Less Than You Earn

Proverbs 21:20 challenges us with this statement: *"There is treasure to be desired and oil in the dwelling of the wise; but a foolish man spendeth it up."* Keep some funds for a "rainy day." Prepare for the day when you are without a church, or the vehicle breaks down, or an emergency occurs. Some give the rule that we should give God ten percent, ourselves ten percent (savings) and live on eighty percent.

Take Care Of Your Possessions
Proverbs 12:27 declares "The slothful man roasteth not that which he took in hunting: but the substance of a diligent man is precious." Stretch the life of everything you possess. For example, neatly hang up your suits when you come home from preaching. Polish the shoes regularly. Keep the vehicle clean. Keep the vehicle serviced regularly.

Don't Trust In Possessions
Proverbs 11:28 warns us that "He that trusteth in his riches shall fall: but the righteous shall flourish as a branch." Major on being rich spiritually.

Avoid Any Purchase Without First Seeking The Blessing Of God
Proverbs 10:22 declares, "The blessing of the Lord, it maketh rich, and He addeth no sorrow with it." Pray about purchases. Count the cost before making a financial deal. Always seek the Lord's will in financial matters. Often financial troubles develop when purchases are made without the Lord's leadership or blessing.

Receive An Inheritance With Wisdom
"An inheritance may be gotten hastily at the beginning; but the end thereof shall not be blessed," Proverbs 20:21 warns. Pay the tithe on the inheritance. Put the rest in a short term investment. Seek the Lord's will about how to spend this gift, rather than unwisely use the money.

Give Liberally Unto The Lord

Proverbs 19:17 admonishes us with these challenging words: "He that hath pity upon the poor lendeth unto the Lord; and that which he hath given will he pay him again." The Lord keeps an accurate record of our giving. As we give for His glory, our needs will be met according to His will.

DEATH, DISABILITY AND SOME OTHER D'S YOU MUST CONSIDER

Some things in life we just don't want to consider. We'd rather put them on the back burner. "I'm young. Nothing is going to happen to me!" Tell that to some women who were made widows at a very young age. The honest, thinking, practical young preacher just may want to consider the following. It is best to repair the roof when the sun is shining. Good health and exuberant life today just may change tomorrow. It is not wise to put off until tomorrow what should be done today. Let me joggle your brain. Young preacher, at least think on these things.

Death

"More preachers die of heartache than a heart attack," someone said. However, young preachers do die! Often young preachers live in parsonages. What would happen to your dear wife if she called 911 tonight and the paramedics pronounced you dead on the floor of that house that is not yours? The pastor's wife would be required to move out to make room for the new pastor and his family. What would your bereaved mate do? Life insurance could meet this financial need. Term life insurance can be purchased fairly inexpensively. How much? Begin with one-hundred thousand, maybe two or three times that much while the children are being educated.

Disability

Lose your voice and you cannot preach, young preacher. Suffer a stroke, or maybe a heart attack, and be laid up for weeks, maybe the rest of your life. Disability benefits from the government usually take months, maybe years, to receive. Why don't you consider a short term disability policy? Or maybe even a long-term policy? The church treasurer is allowed to write the check from your salary provision.

Dividends

Most young preachers live from week to week, stretching the salary just as far as possible. But, most preachers just beginning their ministries, can set aside a few dollars each week for the future if they exercise financial discipline. Begin early; profit later. Begin a savings account. Build it up to a few hundred dollars. Invest in stocks or mutual funds. Sign the reinvestment form and allow the dividends to grow. A monthly contribution to the denomination's pension plan also would be a wise investment. Thirty years of consistent investing will produce a much- needed crop when you come to the end of the ministerial road. In the event of your death, your spouse and children will have some financial security.

Date

Young preacher, your most prized possession should be your mate. Date your mate while you are rearing the children. Don't let the ones God has loaned you stand in the way of your enjoying the presence of your dear wife. Before you know it, the youngsters will be grown. Enjoy your wife's company now. Take her out to eat once a week. Schedule a few days of rest and relaxation once a year without the children. Write her love notes. Treat her like a queen. Remember, we are married for "better or worse." Sometimes the worse invades even a young preacher's home. Be prepared for the rainy days by enjoying the sunshine today.

Dedicate

If the Lord blesses a young preacher and his mate with a child or children, those youngsters should be dedicated to the Lord in the crib. How long will the Lord allow you to have those precious ones? Many young preachers and their wives have buried a child. It behooves the man of God to rear those boys and girls in the ways of the Lord. Spend time with them. Tell them you love them. Do it several times a day. Give that child your undivided attention when he or she wants to vent feelings. That television ball game can wait. Exercise stewardship of your children as if the Lord may remove that child or children from your home any day.

Deed

The young preacher could possibly benefit by locking in a safe place two deeds: the deed to a home and the deed to a cemetery lot. Purchasing a home just may be one of the best investments a preacher may make. But, the smallest piece of land you will ever buy may come in handy if the Lord chooses to remove you from your family's presence. It is never too early to contemplate this purchase. Even if your body is destined for a family plot near the home place, still it may be wise to get a deed

and save your wife this trouble if you are unexpectedly removed from your home.

Gruesome!

Yes, this will not be my most favorite article. However, let's face reality, young preacher. If you don't make these plans and decisions now, it will be too late when death or disability strike. I challenge you to give careful consideration to these words. Your spouse just may thank me a few years from now.

REMEMBERING

One of our grandchildren was riding with me in my vehicle from the home to the church. His father was driving his own vehicle so he could remain at the church and work on the office computers. The grandson was scheduled to begin four-year old kindergarten in a few days. As we were traveling, I noticed that he was saying "Yep" to every question I asked him. So, I proceeded to give him a grandfatherly lecture on why he should say "Yes, Sir" and "Yes, Ma'am" when he went to kindergarten. He listened intently. Arriving at the church, I said, "Now don't forget that you need to show respect to your teacher and principal by saying "Yes, Ma' am" and "Yes, Sir." I asked, "Do you understand?" Without blinking an eye, he loudly said, "Yep."

Our grandson heard but he didn't put my suggestions into practice. I wonder if that is the way we treat what we hear. Once I stopped in a fast food restaurant for a snack. An older man struck up a conversation. After talking a few minutes, he sternly stared me in the eyes and said, "How old did I say I am?" I was startled. And, I could not for the life of me remember his age. He forcefully stated, "Young man, I am 72. Now don't forget that. When someone tells you something, you ought to remember what they say." "Yes, Sir," I exclaimed.

May I remind you of some of the statements printed in this manual?

- Always begin the day with the Scriptures and prayer.
- Be extremely careful when you counsel the opposite sex.
- Carry a mint in your pocket to place in your mouth after you preach.
- Date your wife at an inexpensive restaurant once a week.
- Exercise regularly. Park your vehicle at the far end of the hospital's parking lot. Walk the steps.
- Flirt with no woman! Be devoted to your wife. Write her love notes. Treat her like a queen.
- Give kind, optimistic statements to the congregation. Write thank you notes for gifts received.
- Help the wife around the home, especially when you first move into a new pastorate.
- Invest wisely for the future. A systematic method of saving is essential.
- Judge not. Commit problem church members to the Lord.
- Kill the temptation of laziness. Check off items in your planning book as they are accomplished.
- Love your congregation. Give handshakes, smiles, telephone calls, even to dissatisfied

members.
- Memorize Scripture.
- Neatly hang up clothes in the closet. Buy quality clothes and wear them many years.
- Open your home to missionaries, evangelists, preachers, and other Christian workers.
- Place Gospel tracts wherever you go. Leave church bulletins and booklets in hospital rooms.
- Quit bad habits, like chewing fingernails, using "minced oaths," overeating, etc.
- Refuse to spread gossip. Defend your brother pastor. Get the truth from him.
- Share God's blessings by tithing. Keep a twenty dollar bill in your billfold to assist someone.
- Trust the Lord for victory over pastoral problems. Pray long before acting.
- Unite the congregation around prayer meetings.
- Visit in the hospital with a desire to be a blessing. Dress professionally.
- Witness regularly to the unsaved of the saving grace of God. Pray for converts.
- Expect to stay at the present pastorate just as long as possible.
- Yield to the presence and power of the Holy Spirit in preparation and preaching of sermons.
- Zip off letters of commendation to your congregation. Write at least one note a week.

THE CHURCH

BE ORGANIZED

Being organized is simple. It is necessary. It is productive. Being unorganized is simple, too. Just don't do anything and suffer the consequences. But, the young preacher will experience much more fruit from his labors if he is a preacher who knows where he has been and where he is going. Let me give four easy-to-practice suggestions.

File Folders
Purchase a box of the regular-size file folders. The ones that are divided in three sections may prove to be easier to use. File everything. First, keep file folders near or on your desk. File material that needs your immediate attention in these handy folders. Write on the tab of the folder the contents. As you check the mail, immediately file information that needs your attention soon. Throw everything else in the trash can. For example, upcoming youth meetings, college announcements, meetings at the churches, items you may want to purchase for the church, ideas for church growth or pastoring, etc. — place these in a file folder according to categories as you open the mail. About every month or two thumb through the folders and discard the outdated material.

Secondly, place a four drawer file cabinet near your desk. Establish at least three types of files: theology, information, and church business. Under the theological category, file items from angels to zoology that you may use in sermon preparation, counseling, or providing information for others. These files will grow as you continue in the ministry. Cut out magazine articles, pictures, illustrations, etc. File anything and everything that you may use in the future.

Thirdly, establish a file drawer (or continue the one the previous pastor began) for church business, such as budgets, financial reports, warranties, purchase orders, building projects, etc. Be determined to leave behind clearly identified files of everything the church did when you were the pastor, from baptisms, to new members, to church business items.

Files that are marked on the tab the exact contents will keep you organized today and the rest of your ministry. It will save you much time instead of searching through piles of papers. Organized preachers accomplish more for the Lord.

3 By 5 CARDS
Keep two or three 3 by 5 inch cards in your coat or shirt pocket or pocket calendar book. Write down everything — the prayer request, the person sick in the hospital, the change of address of a church member, a thought for a sermon, an idea for next year's church program, etc. Every week or two go through the cards, record all the pertinent information on one card. Too many young preachers are forgetful. There is much to remember in this fast-paced society.

Pocket Organizer
The colleges distribute them every year. Companies will send you two or three at the beginning of each year. It doesn't matter which type you use — just utilize to the fullest the pocket organizer. I prefer the two year organizer. Some preachers purchase the more expensive ones produced by DayTimer or Franklin.

Record everything in the organizer. From appointments to baby births (name and date of birth) to special church meetings to ground breaking services to vacation days — in other words, place everything you do in the organizer. Keep the used calendar books on a shelf for future reference. Next to your Bible, this should be the most important book you have in your possession all of the time.

Electronic Organizer
Prices continue to decline on electronic organizers. Purchase the type where you have enough room to record the names, addresses, and telephone numbers of church members, family members, and pastor friends. This will prove to be an invaluable asset to your ministry. Keep the information up to date.

Even The Most Organized Can Be Forgetful
The young preacher has many things on his mind, places to go, responsibilities to fulfill, and so much to accomplish for the Lord. Everyone has the same amount of twenty-four hours. It behooves the busy preacher to accomplish as much as possible each day. Set goals, establish plans, and be determined to live every day to its fullest. A 3 by 5 card or a calendar book will not guarantee that the young preacher will not forget an

appointment or fail to visit a sick church member. However, his honest attempt to be organized will assist him to accomplish far more than if he just relies upon his memory.

YOUR DAILY BIBLE READING

When you first enter the ministry, you are overwhelmed with the variety of responsibilities. Teaching a Sunday School class, preaching three or four times every week, visiting, counseling, and on and on the list goes. Besides the challenges of the ministry, you will want to devote time with the wife and children. The lawn must be mowed. The vehicle tuned up. Every day is taken up with demands that extract your time and energy. You go to bed each night exhausted, remembering those jobs that you just did not get accomplished that day.

Your Most Important Responsibility
Having your daily devotions. Your quiet time. Prayer and Bible study. Whatever you call it, a daily spiritual exercise is absolutely essential. Nothing must squeeze out of your busy, daily schedule a personal time of reading the Word of God and praying.

Make An Appointment
Decide the best time to observe your quiet time. Determine where you should meet the Lord. Establish a

schedule. Develop a method. This will demand some trial and error. Your enemy, the devil, will attack you from all directions to rob you of a personal relationship with your God. To carry out a meaningful, daily Bible reading schedule will demand continued determination and self-discipline.

Early In The Morning?
Note in the Scriptures how many spiritual leaders rose early in the morning to accomplish God's will. That may be the best time for the young preacher. Before the family rises, in the quietness of the den or kitchen, meeting the Lord can be a precious time of basking in His love. Or, maybe arriving early in the study before the secretary or associates gather, you could enjoy thirty minutes to an hour of spiritual solitude. Determine the best time for you and stick to it.

A Time Of Devotions, Not Sermon Preparation
Exercise self-discipline and feed your own soul first. Yes, I know, a preacher reading a passage of Scripture can excite his thoughts to begin preparing a sermon. Resist that temptation. Your spiritual battery must first be recharged. Search the Scriptures for personal benefit. Apply the inspired Word of God to your own life. Maybe how that special passage speaks to you could be written in a notebook.

Place A Think Pad Beside You
As you read the Scripture, thoughts of responsibilities you must do will enter your mind. Refuse to ponder on those items. Simply and quickly write down those thoughts on your think pad.

Keep reading. Don't allow those thoughts to detour you from that which is more important — your personal Bible reading. Then when you are finished, place those written down names or items in your calendar book to be acted upon as time allows.

Establish Some Guidelines
Where to read? You should follow a prescribed guideline of profitable Bible reading. On the last few days of December of each year, determine where you are going to read the next year. Maybe you could read the Gospels over and over again for a year. Surely the entire Bible from Genesis to Revelation should be read in a year or two. Some believers read the Psalm and the Proverb that correspond to the date of each day. Maybe you could devote an entire year to the Epistles. Several months could be designated for the reading of the prophets.

Special Reading For Special Seasons
During the month before Easter, read devotionally Matthew 21-28; Mark 14-16; Luke 22-24; and John 17-21. You may want to challenge your congregation to do the same. During the month before Christmas, read Matthew 1 and 2; and Luke 1 and 2. Your congregation could also profit by reading these chapters several times before Christmas day.

Mark Your Bible?
Some preachers refuse to mark their Bible with a pen. Others mark almost every verse. Underlining verses with a colored marker that does not bleed through the pages may be beneficial. Excessive writing or marking could be questionable, especially if you read from your Bible in the presence of those you want to win to Christ. They

might be more interested in your written words and method of underscoring than the verses you want them to read Use the same color of pen. Allow this marking of verses to benefit you when you read those same verses again.

Memorize Scripture
Develop a method of memorizing God's Word early in your ministry. Older ministers just can't remember as well as younger preachers. Write verses on cards. Stick them to the dash of your auto for continued review. Of course, systematic Bible reading will help you to place God's Word in your heart and mind.

Develop A Method Today
Don't let today go by before determining a beneficial, Bible reading program. A "hit and miss" method will rob you of the daily, spiritual blessings that can be yours by systematically reading the most important book in the world — God's Word. Surely if anyone should read the inspired Scriptures with continued, greater understanding, and spiritual profit, it ought to be a preacher!

A DAILY PRAYER SCHEDULE

In conjunction with this personal plan of Scripture reading, it would be most beneficial if you would develop a prayer plan, too. This project will demand even more self-discipline than the daily Bible reading. Therefore, you must determine in your own mind and heart if you really want to pursue a daily prayer schedule.

Determine The Method
If you really want to intercede for your congregation, the missionaries, the unconverted, and other special needs, then let me make several suggestions.

First, purchase your "prayer book." A well-bound, hardback book about the size of your Bible would be a good investment. At least 100 pages will be needed eventually. Remember you will want to use the same book for many years.

On the front page, record your name, address, and the date you are beginning the prayer book. Write as neatly as possible in the book. Maybe you should print.

Divide the book into several categories. Let me suggest the following: Family, Church Family, Unsaved, Missionaries, and Special Requests.

Record the names of your family members on the first few pages. Skip several lines between the names to provide space to record future births and marriages.

Secure all of the names of the members of your church congregation. Put them in systematic alphabetical order. In the Church Family section, record the names from A to Z. Place the last name first. Skip 3 lines between the names to give you space to add additional names of those who become a part of your church family later. Divide this list equally between Monday, Tuesday, Wednesday, Thursday, and Friday.

Third, develop a section for the unsaved. Set aside several pages. Record the names of those you are praying for. When that person is converted, you will want to put a check beside the name and write the date of the decision. For the active, burdened pastor, this list will probably grow faster than all of the others put together.

Fourth, set aside a section for foreign missionaries. Write at the top of the page the country followed by the names of the missionaries serving in that mission field. Skip three lines between the names. Skip three pages between the countries.

Establish a section for home missionaries. Record their names and the place of service.

Fifth, designate a section for special prayer requests that apply to your pastorate and community.

Use The Prayer Book Regularly

After reading God's Word devotionally, open your prayer book. Pray for your immediate family by name and needs. You may want to record specific needs beside their names.

Secondly, pray for the members of your congregation by name and by day. For example, you may want to pray for those whose names end in A through C on Monday, D through G on Tuesday, etc. Possibly you could record specific prayer requests by their names. Write down the date and how the Lord answers that request. As new members are added to the church roll, record those names in the proper alphabetical listing.

Then, pray for the missionaries. You may want to pray for the missionaries in one country on Monday, another country on Tuesday, etc. As the years expire, your list will include deletions and additions. Mark through the names when they leave the field; add the names of new appointees.

Next, pray for the unsaved. This is a page of great excitement. As the unconverted trust Christ as Savior, record the date of their conversion with a big check by their names.

The pages of special requests will be marked probably more than any of the other pages. As church projects are completed, personal needs met, and goals accomplished, record how the Lord met the need in a few words with a date.

The Prayer Book Becomes More Valuable

As prayers are answered, names added or deleted, and dates recorded, your prayer book will reveal how the Lord has worked. James declared, "The effectual fervent prayer of a righteous man availeth much." This personal record of your daily prayer time will become even more personal as the years quickly disappear.

Following this plan assures you of praying for everyone you ought to pray for. Calling upon the Lord on behalf of others by name and need intensifies your burden and concern. Recording the answered prayer is a reminder of our wonderful Lord's fulfilled promises. Those you pray for are encouraged to know that your prayer time includes them by name.

The prayer book will prove to be a personal blessing throughout your entire ministry. If you change churches, you may want to develop a new book.

Some computer programs allow for this planned prayer time to be installed on a hard drive. That may be okay; however, a prayer book developed in your own handwriting can become a very personal and fulfilling means of obeying Paul's admonition to the young preacher Timothy, *"I exhort therefore, that, first of all, supplications, prayers, intercessions, and giving of thanks be made for all men."*

WHEN YOU MOVE TO A NEW PASTORATE

Excitement fills the air when the young preacher and his wife make plans to move to a new pastorate. New visions are dreamed. Greater opportunities to fulfill the call of God prevail. The challenges of preaching, leading, witnessing, and visiting fill the mind. The move is made. The furniture is unloaded. Some of the church members come over. And, now it dawns on the young preacher that "I am the pastor. I am the one the church has approved. I'm it! Oh, Lord help me. Where do I begin?"

Assist The Wife
That's where it begins! As much as the books need to be unpacked, the computer set up, the first sermon prepared, some church members met, and on and on the list goes, the wife must first receive assistance in hanging curtains and blinds, moving furniture, placing pictures, etc. The new home, whether a parsonage or a home being purchased, is the wife's castle. The young preacher is probably frightened of the new, awesome responsibility. The wife is even more afraid. Help her get established first.

Arrange The Study

Books must be unpacked and placed on the shelves. The computer must be placed in the perfect spot. Of course, it must be turned on to see if this marvelous instrument survived the move. So, young preacher, spend a few hours preparing your tools the first few weeks at the pastorate.

Prepare For The First Services

Saturate the sermon with prayer. But, don't expect to transform the church with the first message. It will take several months before the pulpit feels comfortable. Often a new pastor brings out church members who got disgruntled with the previous preacher. Unkind words and actions committed toward the previous pastor may cause some to go the altar. Don't pat yourself on the back, young preacher. Just thank the Lord for the opportunity to preach God's Word. Trust the Holy Spirit to do His ministry among the congregation.

Inform The Congregation

Pastor? Preacher? Brother? The first name? The last name? They will want to know how to address you. Tell them the first week or two, either in the bulletin or by a pulpit announcement.

Study Church Policies

Every church operates differently. Study the constitution and by-laws. Read the minutes. Ask the church clerk for a list of church members (and don't try to purge the church roll immediately!). Ask the deacons how they conduct the ordinances, business meetings, special services, etc. Listen. Take notes. Keep quiet if you don't like what you hear. As the church learns to trust a young preacher, he will be able to make some changes.

Don't Criticize The Former Pastor
Don't even listen to criticism! After staying at a church awhile, the former preacher's action and church operation will be better understood.

Develop Advertising
A new pastor has come to town! Let the community know. Send the information to the local newspaper with your picture. If they will not print it free, you may ask the deacons or finance committee for permission to pay for the advertising. Subscribe to the yellow pages advertising. Produce a neat, informative church brochure. Purchase gospel tracts with the church name, your name, and other information neatly printed on the back. Develop a web page. Purchase several thousand calendars from the Good News Publishers with the church information imprinted. Give one to everyone you see. Introduce yourself as the new pastor in every business. Spread the word that a new pastor has come to town.

Register At Hospitals
Introduce yourself to the hospital chaplains. Request an identification badge if the hospital provides one. Always speak kindly to the information desk workers. Give the hospital personnel the church calendar.

Plan The Church Year
With the assistance of the deacons or the church secretary or maybe the church clerk, determine what the church has done in the last few years on special

occasions. For example, Vacation Bible School, Missionary Conference, Mother's Day, Father's Day, etc.

Visit
If an older church member is available, ask him to take you to all of the homes of the church members. Ask them about their salvation experience. Write down their prayer requests. But, don't participate in their complaints about the previous pastor or a church member. Make the visit optimistic. Pray before you leave.

"Nail The Furniture Down"
Approach this new ministry with the plans to abide in that church just as long as the Lord allows. Yes, discouragements will come. Some people will leave the church. Testing's will abound. But, be determined to put both hands to the plow, look ahead, and trust the Lord for a fruitful ministry.

YOUR FIRST MONTHS AT A NEW PASTORATE

"He that is slothful in his work is brother to him that is a great waster"
(Proverbs 18:9).

Write An Informational Article
Write an informational article for the local newspaper about your becoming the new pastor of the church. Include your picture. Place this information also in the smaller advertising newspapers. Usually you will not be charged for this service.

Get A Business Card Printed
Just a few, maybe 200, at the beginning would be sufficient. Let another minister proof read and evaluate it. When those you visit are not home, be sure to leave your card.

Order Pocket Calendars
One good source for attractive pocket calendars is Good News Publishers, Westchester, Illinois 60153. Get them imprinted with the church's name, address, telephone number, and your name. Most people will accept a calendar that may turn down a gospel tract.

Prepare A Well-Written Brochure
This brochure is to advertise your church. Get a printer that does quality work. Be sure someone proof reads it for grammatical mistakes before you have it printed.

Get Matching Letterhead And Envelopes Printed
Do not order too many at first. You may want to change the copy or style once you learn more about the church and area.

Order Tracts
Install a tract rack at the church to display the gospel literature, called tracts. Select colorful, Biblical, and easy to read tracts. Be sure the church name, address, and telephone number are neatly stamped on the literature. Rather than stamp the information, you may want to order several thousand of the stick-on labels.

Subscribe To The Local Newspaper
Take information to the newspaper about every special event at your church. Write articles to be printed if the newspaper has a Saturday church page. Read the obituary column daily to determine if any of your members have experienced a death in the family.

Use Your Church Bulletin
Use your bulletin to educate members regarding what to call you (pastor, preacher, brother, etc.), your study and visiting hours, your position on standards and matters of convictions, and your goals for the church. Remember that those who do not attend the church services often read a bulletin that is taken home by a family member.

Provide A Form In The Bulletin

Place a form in the bulletin for several weeks for members to list their name, address, employment, telephone numbers, and birth dates. File that information in a computer program, electronic directory, or pocket information booklet. Add to this valuable information regularly.

Yellow Pages

Place an ad in the yellow pages, including church service times and other pertinent information. Often this is a very expensive endeavor. However, newcomers may check the yellow pages, see your church name, and visit in the services.

Learn The Church Members' Names

What a challenge to memorize names, but work on this daily. You and your wife can share information about church members that will assist both of you in learning the names of the church family.

Be Slow To Make Organizational Changes

Preach the Word of God. Love the people. Plan to stay there the rest of your life.

TYPE AND FILE YOUR SERMONS

"My son, let not them depart from thine eyes: keep sound wisdom and discretion"
(Proverbs 3:21).

The sermons the young preacher prepares and preaches, if anointed by the Holy Spirit, are worthy of recording. Material that is neatly placed in notebooks will be of inestimable value.

Purchase A Large Spiral Notebook
Five subject notebooks can be bought on school opening specials at a good price. In that notebook write down all your thoughts and notes as you prepare sermons. Don't be concerned about being neat. When the notebook is full, place it on your study shelf for later reference and begin a new notebook.

Determine The Size Of Paper
Decide on the size of paper you want to keep your sermon notes on. 5 ½ by 8 ½ is a good size. Get a local printer to cut several thousand sheets and punch holes to fit your notebooks.

Purchase At Least Two Notebooks
Purchase the notebook size of the paper the printer cut. Mark the notebooks "New Testament" and "Old Testament." As your sermon material grows you will want to subdivide the books of the Bible and other subjects in other notebooks. In just a few years you will have several notebooks full of valuable sermon material.

Type All Your Sermon Outlines
Type all your sermon outlines and place them in the notebook immediately after they are preached. If you cannot type, learn to type at a local school or use the hunt and peck system. You could get a church member or your wife to type for you, but you remember the material better if you type it yourself.

Record Information
On the back of the sermon outline, record the date and place the sermon was preached. Maybe you will want to record this information also in a computer program or in the back of this manual.

Prepare Separate Notebooks
Prepare separate notebooks for illustrations, funeral messages, and wedding outlines. The material may look lost in the notebook at first, but as the years pass the notebooks will fill up quickly.

Prepare The Sermon Outline For Filing
Prepare the sermon outline for filing before you preach it. If you don't, your delay may cause you to forget to file the material.

Why Notebooks?

Notebooks help you to be systematic and neat in preparation. It provides material at your fingertips for future references. This method assists you in writing your book later in life. Besides, you never can tell — your wife may edit the material, sell it, and provide an income for herself after you die.

YOUR SERMON MATERIAL

Prayer and study give birth to sermons. The hours of heart and mind preparation should not satisfy just one sermon. The material can be typed or neatly printed and filed for future reference.

Prepare Well
Almost every sermon a young preacher delivers will be his first. The ideas, interpretations, illustrations, and outlines should be conserved. You think you are busy now. The older you get, the busier you become. Prepare well now. The recorded material will benefit you the rest of your ministry.

As a young preacher, I pastored a small mission. It fell my lot to lead the singing, teach a Sunday School class, lead a training hour class, and preach twice on Sunday and on Wednesday evening. Besides these challenging responsibilities, the Lord provided the opportunity to conduct a twenty-minute, daily radio broadcast on a local radio station. Raising the funds for the radio broadcast and establishing the church program also fell upon my shoulders. Quite a challenge and I loved every minute of it.

An older minister, pastoring a Bible church in the same city, influenced me to study and preach from books of the Bible. Purchasing several individual commentaries, I studied hours each day, outlining and writing out every word. Some church members typed the sermon material. I preached the expository messages on the radio and from the pulpit.

Use Notebooks
That sermon material was typed on 8 ½" by 5 ½" notebook paper. Notebooks were purchased and divided first into Old Testament and New Testament sermons. Later, notebooks were added to include other divisions of the Scriptures.

The sermon material has been expanded to be placed in nearly two dozen notebooks. When called upon to teach a Sunday School class in the absence of the teacher, the material is usually already outlined. When studying for sermons, previously used material can benefit the preparation. Most young preachers will preach at least one hundred and fifty sermons each year. Multiply that by ten and then twenty as the years quickly rush by. This is valuable material that should not be wasted.

Use The Computer
Today's computer programs allow the young preacher to type his sermons neatly, placing the Scripture verses in the typed text. Rather than use the notebooks, you can save the material in the computer. Then retrieve it by subject, Scripture, date or place preached.

If you use the notebooks, purchase a thousand sheets of the notebook paper from a local printer who can cut them the right size with the holes. Look for the notebooks on sale. Label the outside of the notebooks neatly and clearly.

Surely there is a church member who would consider it a privilege to type your sermons, if you do not type. After the sermon is preached, record on the back of the page and in the computer the place and date of its delivery.

Illustrations
Illustrations should be kept in a separate notebook. Record when you use them. (Congregations don't like to hear the same illustrations over and over.) Thousands of illustrations can be purchased through several computer programs. Books of illustrations are still being produced. The best illustrations are gleaned from the Scriptures. Begin recording those vivid, descriptive illustrations in a notebook. Add to them regularly as you continue to read and study God's Word.

Weddings
Wedding ceremonies should be filed in a separate notebook. You may want to purchase a nicer notebook for this material. Often the pastor's written material is in full view of the congregation. Be sure to record the names of the bride and groom and the date of the wedding. Some couples will request a poem, illustration, or outline months or years later.

Funerals

Funeral sermons should be written out and filed separately. Quite a few people who hear your funeral sermon will request a copy of something you stated. Determine now the method you are going to follow the rest of your ministry. You'll be glad you did.

SERMON RESOURCES

The young preacher must be a preacher! Preaching demands preparation: adequate preparation, Holy Spirit anointed preparation, preparation that produces spiritual fruit. And, such fruit does not just happen. The young preacher absolutely must devote constant attention to sermon preparation. Once one sermon is completed, the mind and heart must begin to plan the next message. Such attention to sermon preparation and preaching can be divided into four essential categories.

The Library
First, young preachers must be readers. Read three books at a time — one in the study, one in the vehicle, and one at home. I personally prefer to underline words and statements with a colored pen. Keep a record of the books read over the life time. Maybe write a few words of description about the book. Read all types of books.

Secondly, purchase books regularly. Not just any and every book, but books that can truly benefit the ministry. Contact pastors for a suggested list. The two-volume work, The Master's Library by Cyril Barber, could be most helpful in establishing a library. Of course, the Bible should receive the major attention. However, commentaries on the entire Bible and on individual books would greatly benefit sermon preparation. By preaching expository sermons, the young preacher would find it beneficial to purchase several books on the book of the Bible or the subject matter. Over a period of years a large library can be developed. Some preachers purchase books of sermons. They may produce an idea for a sermon or a series of messages. "But a sermon is like a toothbrush — use your own," so wrote Floyd Bresee.

The File
A filing system reserves material for use during the entire ministry. File at least these categories:
- Illustrations
- Subject matter from A to Z (such as abortion, divorce, suicide, cults, etc.)
- Bible doctrines
- Current subjects (such as new trends, church music, magazine articles, etc.)
- Personal information (copies of letters, church operation, etc.)

The filing system can be as simple as a cardboard box, as practical as a two or four drawer filing cabinet, or as complex as a computer hardware program. The key to a good system is to be organized. Be able to put your hand on whatever you are looking in a matter of seconds. Filing material on a daily basis will keep the system ready to use whenever needed. (As you open the mail, file that which you may use later. Drop the rest in the trash can.)

The Sermon Notebooks

Some preachers use the index card, others use the 7" by 9" notebook, and others use the 8 ½" by 11" notebook. It really does not matter what size is used just that the young preacher determine the size and stick with it the rest of the ministry. By the twentieth year of preaching, several notebooks will be packed full of sermons. Be sure to write on the back where and when the sermons were preached. Young preachers who preach through books or subjects of the Bible will accumulate hundreds of typed messages quickly. If a Sunday School class needs a teacher one Sunday, the young preacher will be able to turn to the subject matter in a notebook and adequately teach the class.

The Prayer Closet

E.M. Bounds wrote several books on prayer. The young preacher should get all of these books, read them regularly and throughout the entire ministry. The books by Mr. Bounds give excellent direction in sermon preparation. His writings usually bring heavy conviction to the man of God. Practicing his powerful plan surely produces better preachers.

THE LIFESTYLE OF THE YOUNG PREACHER

Just like the first few chapters of Genesis, there are many "firsts" for the young preacher. The first years are learning times. Almost every opportunity is a challenge. And, behind every challenge is a decision. Some preachers just quit. Some change paths. Some stay in despair. But, many others accept the challenges, grow thereby, and develop into productive preachers. Here are six W's to guide the young preacher in the foundational years.

Worship
First and foremost, worship the Lord every day. Call it devotions, quiet time, or whatever but learn to spend time with the Lord each day. Have a consistent Bible reading program, a planned prayer time, and a designated time for personal praise of our Wonderful God. This is the foundation for a satisfying, fruitful ministry. Rise early. Schedule this daily event. Let no one or anything detour you around these moments (or hours) of worshipping the Lord. Here is where spiritual strength is gathered to face the challenges of the day.

Work

Laymen often wonder what a preacher does. Some are bold enough to spew out critical comments about the pastor's workload. So, make up your mind that you are going to stay busy in the work of the Lord. The critical ones will eventually shut their mouths if you devote each day to an active ministry. Arise early. Shower, shave, dress. Go to your study. (If the parsonage is next door to the church, drive your vehicle over to the church parking lot.) Preachers do not punch clocks, but it would be wise to serve as if you are placing a time card in a machine. I read recently that the average preacher works at least 54 hours a week. That should be the minimum time spent in praying, reading, studying, and ministering to the church family and the community. Of course, the man of God is on call twenty-four hours a day, seven days a week. Always be ready to serve those who need your spiritual assistance.

Be Wise

Pray for wisdom. Often the young preacher is pastoring a congregation that has had plenty of experience in "handling a preacher." Usually at least one individual is in the church that feels led of the Lord to keep the preacher humble. Pray first. Speak second. (Don't reverse that order!) Ask the Lord for the ability and knowledge to handle every situation that comes up. It would be wise to think through (ponder) every statement that is made by a church member. Remember that your words and action will usually be repeated. Don't feel that you must give an answer to every accusation, suggestion, or plan. Promise to pray about it. Seek God's wisdom first.

Witness
The young preacher is called to preach, pray, and to present the gospel of Jesus Christ to sinners. Major on the major — winning sinners to Christ. Often the young preacher will major on the minor. Problems will be created! The best method of building a church is to win the unconverted to Christ and train them in the ways of the Lord. So, approach every day as an evangelistic opportunity. Distribute gospel tracts. Talk to people about Christ. Visit with the purpose of evangelism.

Wait
Practice Proverbs 3:5-6. Too often the young preacher will rush into ideas without properly waiting upon the Lord. How many programs have been established by an eager young preacher who failed to count the cost? God's timing is best! A good method of pastoring is to write in your prayer book one year plans, three year plans, and five year plans. Soak these plans in prayer. Seek the Lord's guidance. Then, when you are convinced that the new program or building or idea is ordained by the Lord, take action. It is best to seek the Lord's blessing before the project is begun rather than rush ahead, get into trouble, and then call upon the Lord.

Whistle
Or sing, or pat your foot, to the chorus, "This is the day that the Lord hath made, we will rejoice and be glad in it." Don't get so "bent out of shape" over church responsibilities. Never forget that this is the Lord's work, not yours. It is His church, not yours. Some young preachers get the idea that the work will fall and fold up if they do not have their hands on everything. Nothing further from the truth, young preacher. That

congregation can replace you today and forget about you tomorrow. (Whew! That is a humbling statement, isn't it?) Therefore, go to work with a song in your heart. Whistle or sing while you work. Go home singing. Developing an ulcer, dying of a heart attack, or driving your wife crazy just isn't worth it. The young preacher should be the Lord's servant, accomplishing the Lord's work by the power of the Holy Spirit. Life is just too short to burn the candle at both ends, die prematurely, and be forgotten in a day or two. So, whistle, young preacher, whistle!

Walk
Exercise the mind in the study, the soul in the prayer closet, and the body on the pavement. Walk a mile or two a day. Park on the opposite side of the parking lot at the hospital. Walk the stairs. No one will take care of your body except you, young preacher.

THE YOUNG PREACHER'S APPEARANCE

I believe a young preacher (older one, too) should dress professionally when he visits in the hospital. Once I stood at the information desk of a hospital. Another pastor approached the desk and requested the list of patients. Wearing denim jeans and a tight-fitting polo shirt, the female employee replied, "Are you a preacher?" "Yes," he stated. "Well, you surely don't look like one!"

Professional Appearance
I'm not sure what a preacher is supposed to "look like." However, I quietly agreed with the hospital employee. He was dressed really well for playing golf or fishing, but visiting in the hospital? I'm not so sure. I personally believe that the man of God would be received better if he wore a tie, a suit or a jacket, and matching trousers. (Most salesmen I see in the hospital dress that way.) The pastor represents the Lord and his church at the bedside of a sick church member. Hospital personnel will have more respect for the preacher if he dresses neatly and professionally. Of course, that may not always be possible if he is called in the middle of the night or at another awkward time.

The Words
The young preacher needs to be careful about his words, too. Slang words (such as "gosh" and "darn" which replace God and "damn") shouldn't fall from the preacher's lips. "I swear" is not necessary. "Lord have mercy" may come from the church members' mouths, but the conscientious preacher should be extremely careful about this expression and others that degrade the name of God. When I was a young preacher, I would say "he scared me to death" until a sincere man reminded me that I wasn't dead. Now I'll say, "he scared me half to death." Maybe even that is stretching the truth.

The Breath
And, young preacher, don't just be careful about your words, but also take care of the breath that produces your speech. Offensive breath can turn people away. When you leave the pulpit, place a mint in your mouth. (Maybe you could give your wife one, too.) Always keep a breath refresher of some kind in your pocket. When you witness for Christ or just carry on a normal conversation, the breath should be pleasing, not offensive, to the listeners. And, don't stand too close! Give them a comfort zone.

Be Careful What People See
Once just before walking out the side door to conduct a funeral and onto the church pulpit area, the other pastor told me that he almost hanged himself that morning on his lapel microphone. A smile beamed across my face when I walked toward the pulpit in front of the grieving family. Whew! Did my wife straighten me out after the funeral. Be careful of facial expressions. Even when the young preacher is driving in the funeral processional, he

needs to be careful, remembering that people are observing him. Once entering the cemetery, the pastor on the passenger side stated that there was a "light" buried in the north corner of the cemetery. Puzzled, I just couldn't figure that one out, until he said "an Israelite" is buried there. I laughed heartily. Too heartily. The bereaved saw my actions. So, young preacher, jokes are okay in the right places but at funerals? Well, probably not!

Set An Example
When the ushers come down the aisle to receive the offering ("lift it," some say), I believe the pastor should place his tithing envelope or check in the offering plate. He is setting an example. The congregation is recognizing that the preacher is practicing what he preaches. That's not pride. It is leadership.

Shake Hands
I really believe that every hand ought to be shaken either before or after the services, if at all possible. Personal contact is valuable. Also, the preacher will learn people's problems, fears, frustrations, and blessings while shaking hands. In the age in which we live, many people go to church services with heavy burdens. A hand touch and a kind word from the preacher can relieve much of that ordeal or difficulty.

The Opposite Sex
I do believe though that the preacher, young or older, should be extremely careful about physical contact with the opposite sex. Maybe some preachers can freely hug the necks of the church ladies, but probably most of us shouldn't. Maybe an older lady can occasionally get a

slight hug from the young preacher. However, wholesale hugging and kissing of church members can be awfully dangerous for most of us. Furthermore, the young preacher should be extremely careful about counseling the opposite sex. I have a window in the door of my study where others can easily see, but not hear, the person being counseled.

Once a woman insisted on getting some counseling on Saturday morning. I asked our school principal to go to his office that day. He took his wife and two sons. They walked by my office door several times. Abundant protection!

Your Clothes
Match your clothes. Keep the food off of your tie. Polish your shoes. If you think the shirt is dirty, it probably is. Ask your wife to examine your wearing apparel before leaving the home. Young preacher, stand in front of the mirror and say to yourself, "I am a preacher. God help me to be the very best ambassador possible."

MINISTERIAL ETHICS

Often the young preacher will minister in a church where he serves as "the second man," an associate, or on the church staff in some capacity. This is a position of honor and opportunity. This post provides an excellent privilege of learning how to pastor under the tutelage of a senior minister. But, young preacher friend, there are some rules that must be followed in order to be successful in this position.

Respect The Pastor
You may not always agree with him, but respect him as your leader. The minute you begin to refuse to respect his position, resign and move quickly. Most likely he has played a vital part in calling you to your present responsibility. You are serving because of his confidence in you. Therefore, always treat the pastor with the utmost respect.

Refuse To Criticize The Pastor
Once when an associate ministered with me, a church member one day quietly entered his office. He stated, "I want to talk with you about the pastor. But, don't tell him what I said." The associate stood up and declared, "He is the first one I will tell!" The church member left abruptly.

A young preacher serving with a senior pastor will hear criticism, even plots, against the shepherd of the flock. Never, never should the young preacher listen, encourage, or endorse such criticism.

Uphold The Pastor In The Public
Another associate spoke in my absence occasionally. My wife remarked that he always promoted me from the pulpit. She stated, "You can tell that he is devoted to ministering with you." Members who may not like the pastor love to latch on to comments by an associate that casts a reflection upon the pastor. Young preacher, uplift the man of God.

Pray For The Pastor
Daily call your leader's name before the Lord in prayer. He faces problems, challenges, and decisions that you never know a thing about. "The buck stops at his desk," as President Truman once declared. If you fail in your responsibilities, the congregation holds the pastor responsible. Let him know you are praying for him. Maybe leave a note on the pulpit to that effect. Scribble out a few words of encouragement and slide it under his study door. Let him know that there is at least one church member "soaking" him in regular prayer support. Another associate often wrote me postal cards assuring me of his prayer support.

Do Your Job Well
Most pastors are overextended if they perform their ministries well. Young preacher, don't drop the ball! Give one-hundred percent of your time and effort toward the ministry. Get to work a few minutes early. Stay late, if necessary. Another associate often would come by my

study, stick his head in the door late in the afternoon, and say, "Mr. Wiggs. I'm going home, but is there anything I can do to help you?" I never responded in the affirmative, but that servant's attitude surely encouraged me.

Listen To The Pastor Preach
Give your shepherd complete attention when he is preaching. Look at him! Don't write down what you are going to do next week. Don't whisper to your wife. Keep your children under control. (Learn to do that with a look of the eye.) Remember that your leader is looking to you for moral support. Once it was my privilege to have in the congregation two former pastors. Those older men sat together, on the second pew, and provided a hearty "amen" from time to time. What a blessing! Young preacher, treat your pastor when he is preaching as you would like to be treated by him when you are preaching.

Ask, Don't Tell
"May I have tomorrow off?" "Do you think the church board would consider a raise in my salary?" "I feel sick. May I go home early today?" Ask, don't tell, the pastor. Take your pocket calendar book to his study. Plan with your leader a vacation, family plans, etc. Share with him your needs, but don't expect or demand an immediate response. Your attitude of submission to your leader will go a long way in you two working together harmoniously.

Resign Without Fanfare
If you just can't work with the pastor, or the responsibilities seem to be too heavy, or some in the congregation seem to want you to leave, and you feel compelled to resign. Resign! But, don't write a letter of

resignation criticizing the pastor, or judging the church program, or trying to set the deacons straight. That will not accomplish anything. Just resign! And leave as quickly as possible. Don't try to draw a crowd to your "pity party" and turn them against the pastor, or the deacons, or the program, or some particular gripe. Young preacher, you may need a reference someday. Leave on good terms.

KEEP YOUR MOUTH SHUT!

Almost everything the preacher declares is heard by someone. The average person looks up to the man of God. His words hold value in the ears of the listener. The children listen to learn. Some adults strain to hear every word so they can quote the preacher. People love to tell others what "the preacher said." The young preacher must keep in mind how his words influence the listener and are often passed on to others.

Don't Repeat Prayer Requests
So very often a church member or local citizen will share a personal prayer request with the preacher. Just this very act reveals the confidence people put in the man of God. It is sin to promise to pray with someone about a burden and then forget to pray. Prayer requests are better written down, possibly in a prayer book, and remembered before the Lord as promised. It is unethical to reveal to others the prayer burdens. For people to lose confidence in the young preacher means they will refuse to issue other future requests for prayer.

Be Careful About Revealing Counseling
In this age of marital, financial, emotional, and physical problems, the young preacher will be sought out for

counsel. The best counsel is often just listening. To mention from the pulpit an illustration of someone counseled last week is absolutely awful. Maybe the name is not mentioned, but if the one counseled is in the congregation, that person most likely will never return for any more advice. The preacher is much safer in preaching Biblical illustrations rather than referring to those he has advised in his study. If you keep notes of counseling sessions, be absolutely sure that the written words are kept completely secret.

Should You Tell The Wife?
Venting the feelings about a counseling session may make the young preacher feel better, but how does it make the wife feel? Probably prayer requests, the confession of sins, the personal problems of church members should be kept between the preacher and his Omniscient God. To share everything revealed in the study just may harden the wife against a church member or even the ministry. The man of God must determine within his own soul how much he should share with his mate. He should seek the Lord's guidance. It may be better for the family atmosphere if words of encouragement, challenge, and optimism are uttered. Talking about people and their problems could warp the minds of the spouse and even the children against church members. Remember, so very often that which is shared with you in a counseling session is confessed and the person achieves personal, spiritual victory. God forgives and forgets. So should the young preacher. The wife may have more difficulty in forgetting if she has not sat in the entire counseling session, seen the tears, and heard the confessional prayer.

Tell Preacher Friends?

Sad to say, the young preacher may not be able to share with every preacher his burdens and problems. Remember the three preachers fishing? They began to confess their weaknesses. One shared in confidence his problem of the flesh. The other preacher did the same. The third preacher declared; "My weakness is gossip. I can't wait to get off of this boat!" Ecclesiastical gossip can be vicious. "A lie can travel half-way around the world before truth ever gets his boots on." Most preachers enjoy discussing other preachers. Don't forget that, young preacher. Better to keep the mouth shut most of the time. It may be wise to tell nothing but good. If you can find a preacher who can keep your secrets, then cry on his shoulder. If you can't find one, just be content with sharing the challenges of the ministry with the Lord. Keep your mouth shut! Remember, many people thrive on the bad. Tell what God is doing in your congregation and your life. Testify of a soul that has trusted Christ as Savior. If no one has been saved, give a report of those who are under conviction. Be optimistic!

Tell The Lord

Maybe all of us ought to evaluate our praying. Is it all petitions? Or, do we praise Him Who is worthy to be praised? Possibly keeping our mouth shut on our knees is a worthwhile project. Just listen. Just meditate on the greatness of God. Just sing praises to the Lord. Praying can become a complaining, begging, crying session. Spending quality time on the knees just may demand keeping the mouth shut and the heart yearning for the presence and power of the Lord.

CONFIDENTIALITY

Pastors are entrusted with privileged information that should not be shared with others. The young preacher must learn early in the ministry that this information must be kept confidential. An effective ministry depends upon a trusting relationship between church member and pastor. If a parishioner cannot trust the minister, who can be trusted?

The Long Arms Of Confidentiality
The young preacher must learn to be extremely careful:
- When giving sermon illustrations,
- When preparing members to visit inactive church members,
- When nominating church officers and workers,
- When listening to church members stating the faults of other church members,
- When writing a message in the bulletin or church newsletter,
- When talking with the spouse or a family member,
- When giving prayer requests,
- When conversing with a former pastor,
- When conversing with the incoming pastor,
- When giving advice or counsel over the telephone.

Confidential Information

Often a church member will seek counsel from a trusted pastor. The grieving, guilty member will confess wrongdoing, sin, or thoughts of transgression. The confession should lead to repentance, either in the pastor's study or at a church altar. The Lord forgives the sin. And, we preach that the Lord forgets! So should the pastor. To use the privileged information, even if names are not used, in the pulpit is wrong — may I say, "Sin." I heard one minister say, "Illustrations should not go beyond me." That may be good advice. The young preacher can use himself as an illustration, but going beyond that may be treading on dangerous territory. Pride can creep into the young pastor's mind when he knows something no one else knows. It may build up his ego when he says, "Oh, yes, I know ..." when another church member mentions a brother or sister who has fallen into sin. Better to say, "Let's pray for ____"and leave the discussion at that. If the sinning church member truly repented in the pastor's study then the whole congregation will eventually see a changed life. Maybe even a testimony will come from the lips of the restored brother or sister. I have found that it is better if the sinner testifies of the forgiveness rather than I testify for him.

What Should Be Told?

When someone approaches the young preacher for counsel, that person may say or imply, "You are not going to tell anyone, are you?" It may be wise to declare, "You can trust me; however, if you tell me something that indicates you are going to harm yourself or someone else, then I may be forced to share this information."

Otherwise, the one seeking counsel should be able to trust the young preacher with utmost confidence. But, a word of warning. It would be better if the person only confesses the sin and not the details of the transgression. The young preacher does not need to hear the when, why, where, how, etc. of a sin. Share the Scriptures. Ask the guilty one to confess the sin to the Lord. Lead the person to promise God that he or she will never do it again. Give the person some verses of Scripture to read. Encourage the forgiven sinner to be faithful in church services. And, never, never discuss the confessed sin again unless the person brings it up. Even then attempt to assure the one forgiven that God has forgiven and forgotten. I John 1:9 is the foundational Scripture for repentance. If continued counsel is necessary, it would be best to not discuss the confessed sin but give many Scriptures that assure the person of spiritual growth and victory.

Tell The Wife?
I have made it a practice not to share with my wife what has been revealed to me in counseling sessions. Her relationship to the congregation will be purer and stronger if she does not know what is revealed to her husband in secrecy. But, who does the pastor tell? Probably no one! Remember, the only person in the church who does not have a pastor is the pastor. He must confide in the Lord and leave it there.

Tell The Children?
My wife and I had a policy never to discuss church matters at home. Even when certain individuals were determined to ruin our ministry, we refrained from telling the children. I personally believe that

conversations should be optimistic, upbeat, and challenging at the pastor's table. Too many children in the parsonage turn against the church or the ministry because of such pessimism and criticism that are expressed in the pastor's home.

Tell The Officials?
Some state statutes may require mandatory reporting in cases of child or adult abuse. The young preacher may be wise in seeking wisdom from a local professional counselor about the proper procedures to follow in cases of abuse. Also, young preacher, you may find it extremely helpful and relieving if you refer some people to a professional counselor or a medical doctor.

Sacred Trust
The young preacher will probably hear more confessions of transgressions than anyone else. The successful, fruitful ministry depends upon trust. Once that trust has been damaged, it is almost impossible to restore.

Dennis P. Wiggs | 151
Especially For The Young Preacher

GETTING EIGHT MEN TO DO THE WORK

Someone said that a good leader will not do the work of eight men, but get eight men to do the work. That is the challenge before the young preacher.

My brother-in-law, John S. Craft, was a missionary to Brazil. After serving one term, John told me how he thought mission boards ought to select missionaries. He suggested that the prospective missionary should be placed in a room with several small children and a box of building blocks. The mission board should observe behind a one-way mirror. If the candidate sat down with the children, taught them how to erect something with the blocks, and allowed them to create the building, the board should approve him to be a missionary. If he made something out of the blocks in the presence of the children, the board should suggest that he apply himself to another line of service. Maybe this might be a good standard of approval for ordination councils.

Organize
The young pastor is often called to a small congregation. A medical doctor told me once, "Dennis, if you let them, the congregation will permit you to do everything." That advice was much better than the medication he gave me

for a suspected ulcer. Yes, I know it may seem better to do it yourself. The job will get done and accomplished your way. However, you will find that you can't do everything. The sooner you learn how to organize the congregation, the smoother running the program will operate. For example, decide what jobs need to be performed at the church. Select (or secure through a nominating committee and a church vote) leaders for those positions.

Pray
Jesus prayed all night before he selected the apostles (Luke 6:12). Before you approach anyone for a leadership position, seek the Lord's guidance. Write down the names of the prospective leaders and their responsibilities. Talk to the Lord about those church members.

Seek Counsel
As a young preacher in a new congregation, be sure to talk with an older church member you can trust about your leadership selections. In my first pastorate I put up the names of men I wanted to stand at the front door and welcome visitors to our revival services. That was a mistake. Some of the men on the list had long-standing grievances against one another. Before the meeting ever began I was in hot water. Showing the list to a deacon or two would have eliminated or improved that idea.

Follow Up
After leadership positions are given to selected men or women, be sure to meet with the leaders individually and discuss their roles. Make the meeting short, maybe after a church service. Let them make suggestions before you

dictatorially demand that the positions fulfill certain responsibilities. Pray with the leaders. Then, occasionally meet with them for suggested improvements.

Trust Them
Trusting leaders to minister effectively will demand patience on your part. Pray for the leaders by name. Tell them you are praying for them. Make suggestions kindly. Train the leaders through personal contact, placing a booklet in their hands about their position. Invite them to visit another church to evaluate how that church carries on that particular ministry. Too many young preachers have acted as a "know-it-all," offended church members, and destroyed the possibilities of a well-organized church.

Young preacher, you want to leave the church in better shape than it was when you arrived on the scene. Everything you organize should be for the benefit of the next pastor. Oh, you plan to stay there thirty years! Great! That is an even better reason for organizing the ministry to operate efficiently.

Dennis P. Wiggs | **154**
Especially for The Young Preacher

MINISTERING FROM THE VEHICLE

Depending upon the location of the ministry, the young preacher spends much time in a vehicle. It stands to reason that proper provisions should be readily available to function as efficiently as possible. Consider this inventory.

In Vehicle's Dash Pocket
- City and area map
- Small New Testament
- Gospel literature neatly placed in an envelope
- Small book to read during unexpected interruptions
- Post cards to write a note during delays in travel
- Small note pad with pen or pencil
- Some type of breath refresher
- Travel toothbrush and toothpaste, dental floss, toothpicks
- Small book to keep travel information for Internal Revenue Service filing
- Vehicle registration

In Lighter Tray
- Two dollars in quarters and dimes for emergencies
- Extra set of house and church keys
- Plug for cellular telephone
- Some mints (especially for diabetics)

In Box In Trunk
- Telephone book of surrounding areas
- Flares, flashlight, roll of paper towels, pair of work gloves, cap
- Spare fuses, can of motor oil, fan belt, electrical tape
- Small box of tools

In Billfold
- Emergency information in case of accident
- Health insurance card
- Extra key to vehicle
- Two dollar bill for an emergency (That type of bill you will refuse to spend most of the time.)
- If you are diabetic, a red alert card

In File At Home
- Copies of all credit card numbers, driver's license, registration, title
- Vehicle insurance file
- "In Case of Death" file so your wife will be knowledgeable of all of your personal affairs: insurance policies, birth certificate, list of investments; copy of will, inventory of library, etc.

GO SOUL WINNING EVERY DAY

"A true witness delivereth souls ..."
(Proverbs 14:25).

The young preacher is busy. Preparing and preaching several times a week is a new experience. The study time for one message takes hours. And soon the young preacher can become frustrated.

He wants to witness. He wants to win souls. But all the church responsibilities are new. There just doesn't seem to be enough time in the day. Here are some suggestions on how to be a witness and still get the church responsibilities done:

Gospel Literature
The preacher should keep tracts, booklets, and other information to show the unconverted sinners. Wherever he goes — service stations, restaurants, rest rooms, hospitals, rest homes, homes, jails, shopping centers — he should have tracts at his fingertips. No other tool is more useful to proclaim the gospel. The tract-conscious preacher can distribute hundreds of tracts in a month's time.

The Postal Service
Preachers pay bills, too. They write letters. The young preacher will have dozens of opportunities each month to present the gospel through the mail.

The Bulletin
Bulletins frequently repeat the same information week after week. Once the service ends, it's as old as yesterday's newspaper. The young pastor often must prepare the bulletin. Include a gospel message regularly. Encourage your people to take them home. Mail them to absentee church members. Bulletins are read, even by sinners. Tell them how to be saved.

Witness
Leave seed thoughts with the gas station attendant, the barber, the trash man. The young preacher can see spiritual fruit in years to come by witnessing with compassion to those who cross his path. Take advantage of every opportunity.

Go Soul Winning At Least One Afternoon A Week
Set aside one afternoon to look for prospects. Ask the Lord to send you to the most needed place. You may go from house to house or make designated visits.

Schedule A Visitation Night
Select a night in the week that's best for you and your people. Announce it in the bulletin. Train those who come. And then visit! If only one comes, rejoice. You have doubled your witness. Don't moan over quantity. Major on quality. More sinners are probably won on visitation night than any other time.

Names Of Those I Want To Win To Christ:

1.
2.
3.
4.
5.
6.
7.
8.
9.
10.
11.
12.
13.
14.
15.
16.
17.
18.
19.
20.
21.
22.
23.
24.
25.
26.
27.
28.
29.
30.

MAJOR ON WITNESSING

The young preacher is busy if he fulfills the responsibilities thrust upon him. Preparing and preaching several times a week is a new experience. Church administration can be quite demanding. Organizing the church program takes time and effort. Visiting the older church members and the sick is essential. But, don't neglect witnessing to sinners of the grace of God. If anyone should faithfully witness, it ought to be the preacher.

Witnessing
Sow seed thoughts wherever you go. Witness kindly and wisely to the convenience store clerk, the barber, the delivery person, etc. Take advantage of every opportunity. You can see spiritual fruit in years to come by faithfully speaking to others about Jesus Christ. Community citizens expect a preacher to talk about spiritual things. Jokes, cute remarks, laughing, even crying, all have their place. But they don't often win a sinner to Christ. Invite people to your church. Volunteer your prayer support when someone shares with you a problem. Even kneel and pray in public when a burdened individual shares with you a specific need.

Gospel Literature
Leave a tract with a proper tip at the restaurant. Deposit a tract in every rest room you enter. Place several pieces of the gospel on the printed page in doctors' offices, beauty and barber shops, train stations, airports, etc. Always have gospel literature with you. Tracts should be neat, not torn or wrinkled. Don't write on them. Handle them with prayer.

Gospel Calendars
Good News Publishers (Wheaton, IL) produces a colorful, pocket calendar. It includes the church name and address on the calendar side and a gospel message on the opposite side. It can also be used as a calling card. This is a very effective tool for advertising your church as well as presenting the gospel of Jesus Christ. Very few people will turn down a calendar.

The Postal Service
Witness via mail. Almost every company sends you advertisements with the bill. Pay the bill on time and include a gospel tract in the return envelope.

The Church Bulletin
The bulletin is a very expensive piece of paper unless your congregation takes it home. Take out the form of service (that most people pay little attention to) and include a gospel message. Many unconverted people who refuse to attend your church services read your bulletin. Every week the bulletin should present the gospel in an interesting, challenging way. Pass out the bulletin when you visit shut-ins, hospital patients, rest home residents, prisoners, etc. Make the plan of salvation clear.

Use the printed page to invite sinners to Christ, explain church membership, and the meaning of baptism. Often the unconverted or backslidden who stay home from church services read the bulletin of a family member who does go to the services.

Schedule Visitation
In this fast-paced society, maybe many of your church members will not participate in a night of visiting in the homes of the unchurched. Even if just one or two show up when you schedule this outreach, thank the Lord for those faithful few. Use them as productively as possible. Distribute gospel tracts from house to house. Place in the hands of every participant gospel literature to leave in the homes they visit.

Be sure to faithfully participate in this outreach program yourself. You may discover that more souls are won to Christ on this special night than any other night.

Personal Soul Winning
Get out of that study. Be known as a visiting pastor. Develop a list of unsaved in your community. Pray for them daily by name. Seek them out on a periodical basis. Ask the Lord to personally use you to win sinners to Christ. The citizens in your community should know that if they have spiritual problems, your church is the place to go. You are the preacher to contact.

Develop A Ministry Of Witnessing
Surround the entire church program around presenting the gospel of Jesus Christ to the community. Every program should be a ministry to reach the lost for Christ. Major on evangelism. Don't neglect prayer, Bible study,

counseling, administration, and other pastoral responsibilities. But, keep at the top the driving determination to win men, women, boys, and girls to Christ.

Produce Soul Winners

"Go ye, therefore, and make disciples," the Scriptures declare. Once a sinner trusts Christ as personal Savior, get that new convert into a Bible study. Train the new Christian to be a witness. Explain the verses to use to win a sinner to Christ. Encourage an evangelistic outreach on the job and in the community.

The Most Important

Be careful. You can easily get involved in everything else that seems to be so important. Major on soul-winning. To win a sinner to Christ is just "like being saved all over again." There is nothing more exciting. Let witnessing to the unconverted be a driving force behind your day by day activities.

ESTABLISH A CHURCH AROUND MEN

"Give instruction to a wise man, and he will be yet wiser: teach a just man, and he will increase in learning"
(Proverbs 9:9-10).

Begin A Men's Prayer Meeting
Select the best time to get your men together at the church altar for prayer. Saturday night is best for many. Begin on time. Write down the names of unsaved men or men with spiritual problems. Without preliminaries, use the time to pray. Some men will not come every time, but encourage all men to come some of the time.

Call Your Men Together
Occasionally after a church service, ask your men to meet you in a certain place at the church. Seek their counsel about a decision, share a burden, or ask them to pray about a problem. Meet just a few minutes.

Win Men To The Lord
Pray daily for opportunities to witness to a man about his relationship with God. Tell them that you are praying for their salvation.

Meet With The Men Converts
When a man trusts Christ as Savior, meet with him weekly for Bible study and fellowship. Go fishing or play golf with him. Take the new convert to other church revival meetings. Share Bible truths and principles with him. Train him to win souls.

Plan Fellowships
Retreats, fellowships, cook-outs will give opportunity to teach men how to pray or give a devotional.

Let Your Men Read The Scripture
Post a monthly schedule of men to read scripture in morning and evening services of the church.

Learn The Names Of The Community Men
Introduce yourself to businessmen and community leaders. Give them your calling card. Speak first to professional leaders.

Write Men
Men who perform a job in church ministries deserve a note from the pastor. Men enjoy receiving mail, too. Send them birthday cards.

Visit With Men
Call upon men to visit with you in the hospitals and rest homes. Let them see your compassion for the community. Ask a deacon or a Sunday School teacher to visit the home of an unconverted or backslidden man.

Treat All Men Alike
It may be difficult, but don't show partiality. Shake hands with all the men, even with the man that may not prefer you as pastor.

Commend Men Publicly
Often men do not get commendations at home. Express to men how much you appreciate them, their commitment to Christ, or diligence in church work.

Ask God For A Man's Church
The preacher needs to be surrounded by godly men. As wonderful as church women are, still the church's strength depends on the quality of men who stand with the pastor.

HOW TO BE A BLESSING TO CHURCH MEMBERS

"A faithful man shall abound with blessings"
(Proverbs 28:20).

- Pray for your church members by name daily. If the list is too long, divide it up into days.
- Try to speak to each person who enters or leaves the church.
- Do not show partiality. Treat everyone equally.
- Remember birthdays or anniversaries with a card or telephone call.
- Be especially kind and loving toward children and older people.
- Express sincere sympathy to those who lose loved ones in death. Visit them; send cards; pray for them.
- Love the church members. Ask the Lord to increase that love.
- To those who oppose you, be kind and friendly. You will be glad in years to come that you spoke, waved, shook hands, treated kindly those who opposed you.

- Listen! Talk less than they talk. (Two ears and one mouth should give large enough hint.)
- Preach the Word of God. Preach against sin, but love the sinner.
- Encourage and challenge the congregation, especially on Sunday and Wednesday nights. You are preparing them to face the works of the devil.
- Write them love notes. Express appreciation to those who labor in the church with you.
- When you leave a church, leave it. As much as you love those you gave your life to, allow their new pastor complete freedom to minister without your interference.

YOUR RELATIONSHIP WITH THE WOMEN'S ORGANIZATIONS

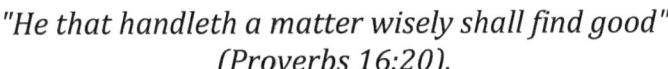

"He that handleth a matter wisely shall find good"
(Proverbs 16:20).

The women's ministry is an effective organization in many churches. They can lend great support to the pastor, lead in missions support and information, and assist in community outreach. The wise pastor will work closely with this group.
- Examine their materials, magazines, programs regularly.
- Encourage them to pursue projects within the purpose and goals of the local church.
- Announce their meetings with enthusiasm and interest.
- Encourage your wife to participate, not lead, in this ministry.
- Visit their meetings occasionally.
- Enlist the women's cooperation in entertaining different associational meetings and guest speakers.

- Encourage the women to present a program of information during the mid-week service at least once a year.
- Do not encourage them to participate in fund-raising projects that solicit funds from the unsaved.
- Publish the officers' names in the church bulletin and newsletter at least twice a year.
- Attend their district, state, and national services occasionally.
- Participate in their weeks of prayer, including their prayer emphasis in the church programs, if possible.
- Encourage the women in soul-winning activities, providing food and clothing to the needy, ministering in rest homes, distributing tracts and the Scriptures, and other outreach ministries.

Dennis P. Wiggs
Especially For The Young Preacher

THINK, BROTHER, THINK

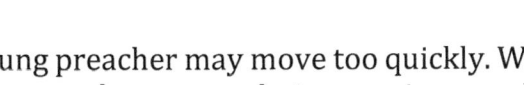

A young preacher may move too quickly. With a desire to please, make a good impression, and accomplish everything thrust upon him, action may be taken too quickly. Let me give a few illustrations with some practical points.

Rushing Ahead Without Permission
The ceiling was low. The sanctuary lighting was poor. One of the deacons suggested that a different type of lighting in the pulpit area would improve that dimly lit area. So, with my encouragement, he bought the ceiling lights, charged the bill to the church, and installed the two lights. Quite proud of his electrical ability, I quickly saw that the job just was not adequate. So, he installed two more lights. Oh, no, that was not sufficient. By this time, the treasurer and the other deacons were asking questions. The deacon who had installed the lights insisted that now the church needed to revamp all of the sanctuary lights. I had to call a meeting. The other deacons kindly rebuked me about running ahead and installing lights without seeking their counsel. There is a good lesson here. Be careful about making changes without seeking the counsel and approval of a governing

body, such as the deacons, a church board, or the church body. Better to preach "in the dark" than to keep the church "in the dark" over building improvements.

Saying The Wrong Words From The Pulpit
Think as you preach, too. I was preaching from the book of Jonah. It was a mission church. The handmade pews were situated on a cement floor and not secured. My wife was expecting a child. She was rather large and uncomfortable. Another church member, also rather naturally plump, was sitting on the same pew. Arms waving, voice raised, I was plowing through the excitement of Jonah being swallowed up by the large fish. The congregation was listening intently until I said that "Jonah was in a whale of a belly." My wife began to laugh, shaking all over. The large lady on the same row got in the act, laughing, shaking until the unbolted pew rumbled like a freight train. The rest of the congregation, who may not have really heard my blunder about Jonah's predicament, began to stare at those two ladies who were now laughing uncontrollably. Brother, you can't preach with an uproar like that. Best to close the message, pray, and go home. So, let me suggest, young preacher, think before you speak. We older ministers have an excuse. Our brain is just tired!

Count The Children
Count the children before you leave the church. The guest minister had preached excellent messages that week at our church. Following the Sunday evening service, he was scheduled to catch an airplane at the local airport, about twenty minutes from the church. Rushing out after the final service, the speaker, my wife, and the children loaded up the small vehicle and headed toward

the airport. We dropped off our guest speaker at the entrance of the airport, telling him we would park the auto and see him off on his flight. Just as I was driving away, one of the children said, "Where's Audra?" She wasn't in the car! I sped back to the church, praying that our fourth child had not been kidnapped, left in the parking lot, or gotten hit by a vehicle. That twenty-minute drive seemed like an eternity! "Pray, kids, pray" was all I could cry out to the wife and children. We arrived at the church. No vehicles in the parking lot. Church lights off. Where is our beautiful, little two-year old, blonde daughter? I rushed into the church. There she stood in the middle of the aisle, wiping her eyes. She had fallen asleep on the pew. "Thank you, Lord!" We rushed back to the airport, parked the car, and walked to the front entrance of the airport. The guest preacher had patiently waited, wondering where that preacher with all of those kids had gone. Young preacher, count the heads before you drive away.

Cold Baptismal Water
Praise the Lord for those who trust Christ as Savior! Excitement was in the services as we made plans to baptize several new converts. The church did not have a baptistry. A creek or river was not available, so, I requested permission to use the baptistry of a church about thirty minutes away. The pastor consented, promising to turn on the water heater after the Sunday morning services. That Sunday afternoon several cars traveled to the church whose pastor had promised warm water to baptize the excited adults and children. In my baptismal instructions I had assured them that the water would be warm.

As the waders clung to my body, the water seemed a little cool. The first convert to be baptized was a lady. You should have seen her eyes when her feet touched the waters of that unheated baptistry. The pastor had forgotten to turn on the heater. What an experience! "Pastor, if that was heated water, I would hate to feel unheated water," several remarked. Young preacher, call ahead, make sure the pastor has not forgotten his promise. Play it safe.

Think Ahead
All of these experiences may seem "funny" now. Let me assure you they were not a bit comical when I traveled through those episodes. Better to think ahead. Save yourself from a lot of difficult circumstances.

MINISTERING TO YOUR CHURCH FAMILY

"Withhold not good from them to whom it is due, when it is in the power of thine hand to do it" (Proverbs 3:27).

Write Thank You Notes
The pastor and his family are usually recipients of generous and sacrificial gifts from the congregation and community leaders. The smallest gift deserves a thank you note. The minister must not be guilty of ingratitude. Some suggestions:
- Keep a record of the gifts and the givers.
- Write a handwritten note within 24 hours.
- Mail the letters. Don't be cheap. Buy a postage stamp in recognition that the gift cost the giver something.

An exception to mailing a thank you note would be if you return a kitchen container of a food gift. The pastor's wife should write a thank-you note and place it in the washed container. Return it immediately!

Write Notes Of Thanksgiving
Observe the spiritual activities of your church members. Write notes regularly to express your appreciation for their faithfulness to the Lord and the church. This includes the nursery director, the visitation chairman, the musicians, and others. Just as you appreciate kind remarks after a sermon, do the same for your church members.

Recognize Your Church Members' Birthdays
Provide the congregation with a form to list the name, address, telephone number, occupation and birth dates of all family members.
- Purchase a large notebook. Record birth dates by months and days.
- Set aside a certain day each month to write the birthday cards for that month. Write the date to mail each card in the place to affix the stamp. Place the cards in order of the date to be mailed. Put a stamp over the date when you mail the card.

Use People's Names
In the bulletin and newsletter, recognize those who serve faithfully in different church responsibilities. Try to use everyone's name at least once a year. For example, commend nursery workers, ushers, custodians, musicians, those who read the Bible through in a year, etc. Of course, try to spell the name correctly.

Love Your People
Show love by respecting them, treating them as members of Christ's body, and being kind even if they don't express the same love to you. Shake the hands of (or wave to) those who may want you to resign as pastor.

Don't Neglect Your Own Family
The pastor can become so busy ministering to others that he neglects his wife and children. If your wife plays the piano or organ or sings specials or is in the choir, write her a thank you note. Express your appreciation privately to your children for their ministry in the church. Remember, you are their pastor, too.

Dennis P. Wiggs
Especially For The Young Preacher

DECISIONS A YOUNG PREACHER MUST FACE

The young preacher should determine his beliefs, practices, and convictions early in his ministry. These should be established before decisions must be made. As you face decisions, pray while you search the scriptures, seek counsel from older ministers, and use common sense. Some decisions may be changed as you progress in the ministry.

Here are some decisions that you will most likely have to determine early in the ministry.
- Will I conduct a wedding ceremony for a Christian and an unbeliever? A divorced person? A couple of different races? Will I conduct a wedding on Sunday?
- How will I handle the funeral of one who belongs to a fraternal organization?
- Will I purchase insurance? How much?
- Should I establish a retirement program?
- Had I rather live in a parsonage or purchase my own home?
- Will I join a ministerial association?
- Will I secure employment outside of pastoring?
- Will my wife work outside the home?

- Should I wear conservative black or blue suits most of the time?
- Should I limit my vehicles to the color black or blue?
- Can I run for political office? How much will I cooperate with local politics?
- Should I accept an honorary doctor's degree?
- Should I travel on Sunday? If I do, should I try to visit other church services?
- Should I eat at restaurants on the Lord's Day?
- Should I patronize a business that sells alcoholic beverages?
- What version of the Bible should I use from the pulpit?
- Can I take a vacation to the ocean? If so, would it be okay to take another couple?
- Should I continue in the ministry if my wife or children rebel against the Lord?
- Should I own a television?
- Should I subscribe to an Internet service?
- Should I send my children to a Christian school or public school?
- Should my wife and I home school our children?
- How modestly should I dress when I mow the lawn at my home?
- Would joining a country club, health club, etc., hurt my testimony?
- Should I participate as a volunteer fireman?
- Should I purchase stock in a company that sells alcoholic beverages?
- Should I always wear a jacket and a tie in the pulpit?

BE A FRIEND TO PREACHERS

"A man that hath friends must show himself friendly"
(Proverbs 18:24).

Defend Other Preachers
Don't be guilty of believing the "ecclesiastical garbage" that is so often spread about other preachers. Personally ask the preacher if such gossip is true. Get the facts from him.

Pray For Other Preachers
Make a list of those you want to pray for regularly and place it in your Bible or prayer books. Tell them you are praying. Write them occasionally. Such a contact just may be what the man of God needs on that certain day. Don't let your youthfulness hinder encouraging an older minister.

Tell Other Preachers
Tell other preachers you are praying for them. Each Sunday morning select a different preacher. Call him about 9:00 A.M. to say that you are praying for him on that particular Lord's Day. Call his name in prayer from your pulpit.

Invite Preachers To Your Home
Take the initiative. Don't wait for others to invite you to their homes. Have them over for a meal or a time of fellowship.

Send Preachers Cards
Recognize his birthday, anniversary, or his illness or bereavement with a card.

Give Money To Preachers
Fellow preachers experience financial difficulty. Assist them with a $10 or $20 gift.

Listen To Preachers
Don't dominate the conversation. God gave us two ears and one mouth -- that should be a big enough hint. Ask the preacher a question, especially the one who is discouraged, and then listen intently to his conversation. Don't brag about God's blessings upon your pastorate if the preacher in your presence is discouraged.

Treat Preachers The Way You Want To Be Treated
The young preacher wants respect, appreciation, and kindness. Treat other preachers the same way. Yes, some preachers may "get on your nerves," but be as kind as possible.

Be A Pastor
The only person in the congregation without a pastor is the preacher. As a young preacher, be a pastor to another preacher. He needs your counsel, fellowship, and concern. When a fellow pastor has been voted out of his pastorate, invite him and his wife for a meal, send them a card of encouragement, and regularly call him on the

telephone with words of encouragement. Minister to the minister.

Preachers I Want To Pray For:

1.
2.
3.
4.
5.
6.
7.
8.
9.
10.
11.
12.
13.
14.
15.
16.
17.
18.
19.
20.
21.
22.
23.
24.
25.

THE CHURCH BULLETIN

One of the most effective tools for keeping the congregation informed is the Sunday bulletin. The pastor uses it to teach, train, challenge, warn, and motivate his flock.

However, a bulletin worth taking home cannot be prepared late Saturday night. Sunday morning's printed page can be a planned, well laid out piece of literature that benefits the worshiper the entire week.

Determine The Style Bulletin You Want
Choose between the color-pictured bulletin with your church name printed on front, the printed form with the church picture on front, or the plain sheet of paper. Some churches give the worshipers the opportunity of recording sermon notes on the back of the bulletin.

Collect Sample Copies From Other Churches
Be sure to keep these on file. Much is learned by observing other bulletins.

Place A File On Your Desk For Bulletin Information
Regularly put news, names, information, and announcements, etc. in that file. Leave nothing to memory.

Purchase Bulletin Cut-Outs
Pictures, scripture, and sayings add to the bulletin. However, don't overuse. Some computer programs provide excellent pictures.

By Thursday, Lay Out The Bulletin On A Blank Sheet Of Paper
Arrange information and pictures for clarity and interest. Let someone proofread the layout.

Use Names In The Bulletin
List the nursery workers, ushers, Sunday School teachers, workers, deacons, etc.

Recognize People
School, civic, community, and church awards should be placed in the bulletin.

Keep The Congregation Informed
List the week's activities. State coming programs and special services. Include a calendar of the month's activities. Print the church budget and gifts at least monthly.

Include Material Of Value
A poem, illustration, sermon outline, puzzle or quiz will motivate many to take the bulletin home.

What Can You Leave Out?
Is the church name used twice? Is the order of service necessary? Why print the nursery list if the schedule is on the nursery door? Are ushers' names essential if you use the same ones every service? Is it necessary to list service times every week? Evaluate the bulletin. Get the most material for the space allotted.

Consider Using Large Print
Different print size and style are attractive and helpful. Older people appreciate the larger print.

Encourage The Congregation To Take The Bulletin Home
Ask them to tape it to the refrigerator for a week and then file it. Extra bulletins should be distributed by visitation teams. Ask a volunteer to mail bulletins to college students, armed service personnel, shut-ins, and delinquent members.

Set A Goal To Produce A Well-Accepted, Used Bulletin
Don't waste time producing a piece of literature that members find no use for two minutes after reading it. The bulletin can be a means of accomplishing much more than announcements or pleas from the pulpit.

Dennis P. Wiggs | 190
Especially For The Young Preacher

SOME WAYS TO IMPROVE THE MID-WEEK SERVICES

Church members attend mid-week service tired, often discouraged, and in need of a spiritual uplift. They endure heavy traffic, rush home from a difficult day on the job, and at times miss the evening meal. Children have homework or a bad report card. Family problems may surface on the way to church.

Financial and physical burdens may weigh heavily on the believer who feels obligated to attend the mid-week church service. Possibly Bible reading and prayer have been neglected. An unconfessed sin could bother the conscience.

The young preacher should recognize the circumstances of the mid-week worshipers. Provide a spiritual oasis in the middle of the week for those who are hungry, thirsty, and weary.

Begin The Service On Time; Conclude At A Reasonable Time
An hour service is long enough for families with small children who need a good night's rest to prepare for

school. A well-planned service can accomplish much in one hour.

Select Hymns Prayerfully And Deliberately
Sing hymns on a certain subject. Buy books that give the history of hymns. Share these interesting accounts with the congregation before you or the music director lead the hymns.

Change The Format Occasionally
Make announcements at the beginning or ending of the service. Sing the middle stanzas of the hymns. Let each person stand and read a favorite verse from Proverbs or Psalms. Sing the first stanza of the hymns without using the hymnal.

Read Missionary Letters
Let one of your members give a five-minute report on a certain missionary or mission field each week.

Ask For Testimonies
Encourage the worshipers to give a testimony. Or better still, select certain ones several days ahead to give testimonies on certain subjects — tithing, prayers answered, soul winning, etc.

Schedule Special Music
Use children who are just beginning to play the piano or organ to play the offertory. Establish a schedule when they will play so they can practice several weeks. If children are learning to play other musical instruments, place them in the schedule. This will boost your attendance plus give the young people an opportunity to learn to play before the public.

Ask The Congregation To Sit In Different Pews
Because most people sit in the same pews, request that they sit in a different pew for just one service. Ask entire families to sit together. Ask each person to introduce himself (some in your congregation may not know everyone). Ask each person to shake seven hands before leaving the service.

Prepare Your Message Well
Give those hungry, thirsty believers something worthwhile to help them face the rest of the week. The mid-week service should be a spiritual oasis in the middle of the week.

The preacher sets the pace for the mid-week service. It is your obligation and opportunity to pray, prepare, and plan to provide your flock with one hour of spiritual nourishment they so desperately need.

HOSPITAL VISITATION

Some Don'ts
- Don't sit on the bed.
- Don't stay too long.
- Don't talk about yourself.
- Don't quote Romans 8:28.
- Don't visit if you are sick.
- Don't stand on the oxygen tube.
- Don't tell the nurse the patient's illness.
- Don't ask the nurse to check your blood pressure.
- Don't eat the patient's food.
- Don't volunteer to move the patient back to bed.
- Don't pray for the Lord to punish the patient even more.
- Don't inform the patient's family that he probably won't live through the night.
- Don't tell the patient about someone who died with the same illness.
- Don't ask the sick person how much the hospital room is costing each day.
- Don't tell a joke when the sick one is in pain.
- Don't fall asleep sitting in the chair.
- Don't keep saying you have to leave and continue to stay.
- Don't sneeze on the patient's food.
- Don't forget to pray.

Some Do's
Visiting the sick church members in the hospital is a responsibility and a pleasure for the young preacher. You should attack this challenge with great enthusiasm and vigor. Hospital visitation is a wonderful opportunity of ministering in the name of Jesus Christ, showing His love, and reaping a bountiful harvest. Do accept this pastoral responsibility with a determined purpose to be a blessing and produce spiritual fruit.

Visit With A Plan
Write the names of those to be visited in a small book. Keep their names, praying for them even after they leave the hospital. In church services when you learn about those who have been placed in the hospital, immediately record the names in your small hospital visitation book. Ask your church congregation to keep you informed.

Visit With A Purpose
Sick people have not only physical needs but spiritual burdens. Read or quote Scripture. Pray. Promise your continued prayer support. Once I read Psalm 23 to a lady in a coma. When she amazingly came out of the deep sleep, she stated that the only activity that she remembered in the intensive care unit was my reading the twenty-third section of the Psalms.

Visit With Patience
Yes, you are a preacher, but, respect the hospital's rules. Wait until the doctor leaves the room. Detain your visit while the nurse dispenses the medication. Exercise your pastoral privilege with care and concern.

Visit With Preparation
Appropriate gospel tracts, booklets, and church literature should usually be left in the hospital room. Because many patients are so heavily medicated that they may not remember your visit, be sure to leave behind your card or church brochure.

Visit With Personal Care
Place a mint in your mouth, assuring your breath to be pleasant. Park your automobile as far away as possible and walk the steps to provide exercise for your body. Always visit the rest room before leaving the hospital to wash your hands. Take vitamin C and gargle with a mouthwash. This may help to ward off germs and illnesses, some say. As you get older or experience physical problems, be sure to take the flu shot annually.

Visit With Perception
It is possible to exaggerate the illness of a church member. The young preacher may feel qualified to play doctor as he visits often in the hospital rooms. That's dangerous. It is best to be the preacher/pastor and minister to the spiritual needs of those who need you so very much.

Visit, Producing Spiritual Fruit
Some patients will trust Christ as Savior. Others will renew their vows to the Lord. Many will become more committed to Christ as they travel through an illness. Still others will learn to cope successfully with a terminal illness. The young preacher can have a vital part to play in these eternal decisions. With a small New Testament in his hand, a notebook to record the names of the

patients, wearing appropriate clothes, and a prayer in his heart, you will find hospital visiting productive and fruitful.

WHEN YOU ARE INVITED TO PREACH AT ANOTHER CHURCH

Another pastor may ask you to conduct a revival meeting or preaching conference at his pastorate. Consider this an honor. It is a wonderful privilege to preach the Word of God at another church. But, it is also an awesome responsibility. The young preacher should turn down this opportunity unless the following can be executed.

Pray
Seek the Lord's guidance in the messages you should preach as the visiting preacher. Proclaiming sermons previously preached may be appropriate; however, that congregation deserves your best. Anoint the messages in prayer. Type or write the sermons again. Prepare the heart, mind, and soul for this great challenge.

Prepare Well
Leaving town for a few days demands preparation. Make a list of everything that must be done before departing. Check off the items as they are accomplished. Who is going to teach the Sunday School class, preach in your absence and prepare the bulletin? Who will be given the

telephone number of the pastor so church members will know where to call in the case of an emergency? Stop the mail and the newspaper if your wife is not going to stay at home.

Prevent Misunderstandings
A few days before the meeting is scheduled, call the pastor to confirm the date. (How many preachers have shown up a week early or arrived too late?) Write down the exact hour the pastor expects you for the first service. Are you expected to eat a meal before the first service? Write down the time. (You may be young, but even young preachers forget.) Get the exact directions to the church, parsonage, or restaurant. Plan ahead. Leave in plenty of time, considering heavy traffic or auto trouble. (That pastor is somewhat nervous anyway, knowing that you may not show up on time for the first service.) Better to be early for this important engagement.

Pave The Way For Good Relations
Visit with the congregation before and after the services. Put a mint in your mouth. Shake hands. Learn names. Be friendly. Smile.

Preach With Wisdom
Use some good old-fashioned common sense. Preaching to a new congregation is difficult for them and for the preacher. Preach the Word! Refrain from making statements, telling jokes, or giving illustrations that may offend someone in the congregation. Remember, you have been called to that church to edify the saints, evangelize the sinners, and encourage the weak. Do just that!

Promote The Pastor
Some well-meaning sister or brother may approach you about a church problem or a dissatisfaction with the pastor. Refuse to get involved! Brag on the pastor (in a reasonable way, of course). Defend him, if necessary. Speak well of him. Never make any statements that may cast a reflection upon the shepherd of that flock.

Present Yourself Willing
Daily be willing to visit with the pastor. Be at his beckoning. Be a servant to his plans for the day.

Practice Ethics
Refuse to sit up late and talk with the pastor about the church problems. Refrain from being a "Mr. Know It All." Get a good night's sleep so you can face the next day with alertness. Don't sit up late and watch television. Spend time in the room provided for you in prayer and sermon preparation. Don't flirt with the pastor's wife or his daughter. Hang up your clothes in the closet. Make up your bed. Take a good bath daily. Take out small portions of food, begin to eat last, eat slowly, and refuse to be a glutton.

Pray With The Pastor
Maybe the pastor doesn't mention praying together, but somehow encourage prayer at the church altar sometime during the day. Bathe the services in prayer. If the pastor does not encourage such actions, be sure to meet with the Lord in privacy on behalf of the services and spiritual fruit.

Proclaim God's Word For Decisions

Preaching God's Word as a guest preacher gives you the opportunity of ministering to people who have problems. Bible preaching reveals sin. Anointed sermons produce spiritual fruit. Therefore, give invitations. Trust the Holy Spirit to bring conviction. Don't try to do the work of the Holy Spirit, but pray and believe in commitments that produce changed lives.

Praise The Lord

Preaching at other churches may prove to be spiritually fruitful. Praise the Lord for the results. Refuse to praise self! The preacher is just a tool, a vessel, a channel. Rejoice in the Lord's blessings. Reject pride. And, return home exalting the Lord for the privilege and honor of preaching God's Word to another church congregation.

LOVE YOUR CONGREGATION

One of the great responsibilities for the young preacher is getting along with people. Christians are human beings. Human beings possess unique and different personalities. And, the young preacher must learn to work with everyone without offending or compromising. What a challenge! You will never please everyone all of the time. Don't even try. However, it would be beneficial to the ministry to set a goal of ministering to the congregation just as effectively as possible.

Love Them
Jesus declared, "*Love one another; as I have loved you, that ye also love one another.*" (John 13:34) Remember the disciples that requested seats of authority? The other disciples were angry and jealous. Remember Simon Peter proudly declaring that he would never deny Christ? Remember Judas Iscariot jingling the betrayal money in his purse at the Last Supper? Remember the disciples forgetting about the miracles of feeding the 4,000 and 5,000 and then questioning Jesus how He would provide their needs? Hard to love such stubborn, faithless, myopic followers. But, Jesus loved them. He commanded us to love the same kind of people.

Some church members are just like the twelve apostles. Inconsistent. Weak. Double-tongued. Unfaithful. Love them anyway! First, remember that the young preacher is not perfect. It may take just as much grace for the congregation to love the man in the pulpit as for him to love those in the pews.

Love Them Anyway
In every born-again believer is value. Maybe even the Lord cannot change some habits and idiosyncrasies of His children. But, He continues to work on them. The young preacher must love those in his congregation as they are. Tolerate the loud, demanding board member. Pray more fervently for the backsliding young believer. Visit anyway the complaining, disgruntled widow. Try to shake everyone's hand. Give a smile, even to those who look the other way. Wave. Exercise the determination to aggressively treat everyone with the same respect.

Some Suggestions

- Pray regularly for all of your flock. Divide equally the membership list in five equal parts. Pray for the first group on Monday, the second group on Tuesday, etc.
- Speak to everyone. Before and/or after the worship services, try to shake everyone's hand and give a kind greeting.
- Visit. Yes, I know ladies work outside of the home and people work on different shifts. But, try to spend a few minutes of fellowship with each church member at least once or twice a year.

- Pray over the telephone when church members call about a burden or a blessing.
- Be with your church family when they face surgery, death, or disappointments. Attend the weddings. Rejoice with them over a new job or a promotion. A young preacher will touch the lives of every church member in some special way in just a few years.
- Consider recognizing birthdays, anniversaries, spiritual birthdays, births of babies, sicknesses and deaths with a card. Mail it to their home.
- Speak well of your flock. Criticism or condemning words will not accomplish anything. Be careful how you make cutting remarks to other preachers about the sheep the Lord has given you.
- Tell them "I love you in the Lord."
- Love without physical affection. Be careful of your contact with the opposite sex. Learn to love everyone spiritually without being physically attracted.

Love Without Partiality
People can be jealous. The young preacher should be careful about giving more attention to some more than others. Try to treat everyone equally. Shake hands on one side of the church this Sunday and on the other side next Sunday. Visit without discrimination. Preach to both sides of the congregation. Exercise genuine love to all groups in the church.

Is It Possible?
Yes, it is possible to love even the unlovely. The Lord can work a special grace in our hearts. In fact, even a casual reading of I John will reveal how important it is for believers to love not only their friends, but even the enemies. Young preacher, everyone in the congregation may not treat you with respect. They may never do anything for you besides attending church services. However, ask the Lord for the grace and strength to prove your love for those the Lord has placed in your watch care. Love your congregation. And, watch that love grow as you remain at that church just as long as the Lord allows.

RECOGNIZE CHURCH MEMBERS' BIRTHDAYS

Collect The Data
For several weeks, prepare a bulletin insert to collect the name, address, and birth date of every church member and child. You will need to do this at least every year to update newcomers. This information should be placed in a large, well-bound notebook. Write January 1 on the first page, January 2 on the second page, all the way to December 31 on individual sheets. Then, record the names on the birthday sheets in ink. Write the addresses in pencil. Utilize each line, leaving enough spaces for future entries.

Purchase The Birthday Cards
Buy the birthday cards by the boxes, possibly a year's supply at once. Often local Christian bookstores will sell them at a discount if you purchase ten or more boxes. Shop the sales on cards. Select cards for children, men, and women.

Begin To Send The Cards
Once or twice a month, devote several hours to writing the cards. Include personal comments in the cards to encourage church members who are bereaved or sick.

Take advantage of this opportunity to express appreciation to faithful church officers. Provide challenging words to young people.

Plan Ahead
Plan to mail the card two or three days before the person's birthday. Write that mailing date where the stamp will be placed. Put the cards in a convenient spot where you can be reminded each day to mail them. Place the stamp over the penciled date where you wrote the mailing date.

A Silent Ministry
Don't comment about this ministry from the pulpit or in conversation. When people thank you for the card, just say "you are welcome." Try to make as little fanfare about this method of recognizing your congregation as possible. This is a personal communication to church members and their family members. Each card will include a different message.

Make Mistakes Graciously
You will not get all of the birthdays recorded the first year. Add them to your notebook as you learn of the omission. You won't need to apologize. Names may be misspelled occasionally and the receiver of the card may correct you publicly. Smile, correct the spelling, and be sure to spell the name correctly next year. Some will reject the birthday cards. Send them anyway. (If you don't, they may criticize you. Yes, people are "funny.") You may send a card on the wrong day. Mark that mistake down as a learning experience and correct the date for proper mailing next year. And, be sure to place your return address on the cards.

Use Your Computer

Once you adequately secure the birthday records, you may want to produce mailing labels. You could include "Happy Birthday" on the label above the name and address. You may want to install a program that will print out the list of birthdays each month.

Make The Cards Personal

Some companies promote birthday cards already embossed with a message and your name. I personally feel that the cards need to be in your handwriting to be effective. This is a wonderful method of communicating with your church family kind statements you may not be able to express in conversations. Everyone loves to get mail. This tool of encouragement will produce excitement and appreciation by those who receive your cards. Often your card may be the only recognition of a person's birthday on this very special day.

Don't Expect Personal Recognition

Probably very few church members will recognize your birthday. Perform this card ministry without looking for personal reward. Realize that most church members do not send cards. Many don't know how to respond to their birthday being recognized. Just exercise this part of your ministry as "unto the Lord." He knows why you are spending the time and finances. As good stewards of our calling, our Lord will reward us properly and in His own time.

ENCOURAGE MISSIONARIES VIA E-MAIL

Many overseas missionaries have access to a telephone line. Most, if not all, home missionaries purchase telephone service. However, overseas telephone calls are awfully expensive; even calls in the states can run up a bill. Letters (snail mail) often take several days or weeks to be delivered. The new method of communication to missionaries is e-mail (electronic mail). The electronic messages are sent between computers that are stored until read. And, what an exciting way to communicate!

Young preachers who own a computer and subscribe to an electronic mailing service should take advantage of this efficient technique of conveying messages. Now, preachers are able to communicate with home and foreign missionaries in just a few seconds via e-mail. Missionaries are able to transmit emergency prayer requests. This new service is a more efficient method of "talking" to those who may need to hear your "voice."
It is not necessary to pay a monthly fee to the World Wide Web. E-mail services are available without cost.

Secure Directories
Directories are produced by the foreign and home missions departments. Colleges and other institutions

develop e-mail directories. The booklets or electronic lists give all the information you need to begin sending messages electronically. Check the latest directories. Enter the names of the missionaries in your e-mail address book.

Recognize Special Events

One of the best reasons for communicating with the missionaries and their families is to recognize their birthdays or some other special event. Preachers are not known for their letter writing. However, e-mail makes it easy. No envelopes. No stamps. No concern about the handwriting. Just zip off a few words of "Happy Birthday," "Congratulations," "Thank the Lord for your faithfulness," etc. The mission's directories provide all of the needed information.

E-Mail Ethics

Keep it short. State your reason for writing in a few words. As e-mail develops, the electronic mailboxes get stuffy. Often "junk mail" clogs up the telephone lines just as your own mailbox collects unwanted or unneeded mail. Learn to write the missionaries in just a few words, expressing your appreciation for their ministry, assuring them of your prayer support, and sharing with them what the Lord is doing in your life or church.

Receive Mail Gladly

Missionaries are using the electronic mailbox as a way of informing supporters about specific prayer requests. Print these requests. Share them with your congregation. Personally take them to the Lord in prayer during your prayer time.

Don't Expect An Answer
Electronic letters are not "fan mail correspondences." Remember how busy the missionary is. Refrain from asking him or her questions that demand research or preparation. And, if you really do need a question answered about the missionary's ministry, be sure to be patient and wait for the answer.

Be Careful What You Say
Remember, mail delivered electronically may not be personal. Being careful what is said is good advice even with our conversations, but especially true when words are recorded in a computer's hard drive.

Sign Your Name And Address
Some e-mail addresses are quite ambiguous. It is better to state your name and full address at the bottom of the letter. Don't demand that a missionary guess who you are and where you pastor.

Produce An E-Mail That Is A Blessing
Missionaries are often lonely ambassadors. An inspiring message on a computer screen may be just what he or she needs. Share verses of Scripture that have been a blessing. Even a rib tickling joke may be challenging. Maybe a sermon outline, or a quote, or a poem could be an encouragement for that faithful servant of the Lord struggling to keep that mission church open. Use the computer as a tool of spiritual blessing.

Dennis P. Wiggs
Especially For The Young Preacher

THE PRAYER MEETING

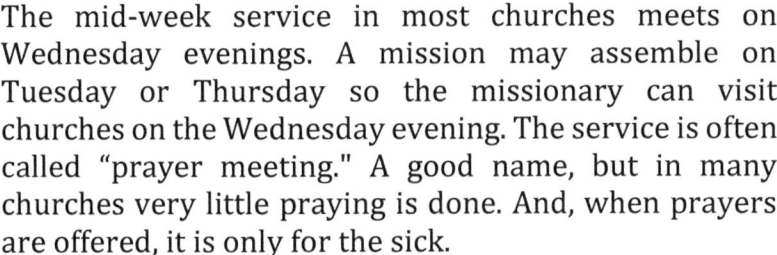

The mid-week service in most churches meets on Wednesday evenings. A mission may assemble on Tuesday or Thursday so the missionary can visit churches on the Wednesday evening. The service is often called "prayer meeting." A good name, but in many churches very little praying is done. And, when prayers are offered, it is only for the sick.

If the mid-week service is going to be labeled "prayer meeting," then shouldn't we practice just that?

Please allow me the opportunity to offer some suggestion to make the mid-week service truly a meeting of prayer. I'm sure other pastors could offer many other suggestions.

First, promote the mid-week service as a family meeting. Provide a program for the children. Several organizations offer challenging programs for boys and girls, even teens. Try to dismiss by 8:30 P.M. so the school children can be taken home in time to get to bed at a satisfactory hour.

Second, squeeze as much as possible in an hour. For the adults, who usually meet in the church sanctuary, two hymns, an offering, a few testimonies, and a short message can be conducted in thirty to forty minutes. Spend the rest of the time in prayer.

Third, there are numbers of ideas on how to conduct profitable prayer time. The pastor is usually the leader. He should spend preparation time to lead the congregation in a rewarding session of prayer. Here are a few suggestions.

- Conduct a sanctuary prayer session. Before prayer needs are made available, the pastor could designate several believers to pray at the conclusion of the request time. They would pay better attention to the requests. Then, ask for prayer requests that involve physical needs. Write down the names and the needs. Second, ask for spiritual prayer requests, such as the names of the unconverted. Third, give the names of several missionaries who have specific needs. Fourth, receive other types of requests from the congregation. Then, ask everyone to come to the church altar or kneel right beside their pew. Call on the designated ones to lead in prayer. The pastor could close in prayer.

- Conduct a separated prayer session. Ask the choir members, nursery workers, and ushers to go to three different classrooms. Designate someone to be in charge of the prayer session. The remaining people could stay in the sanctuary. Prayer requests could be taken. Then, divide the men from the women. Let the women go to the altar and the men go to the rear of the sanctuary.

- Another effective prayer meeting can be accomplished by asking the Sunday School classes to assemble in their classrooms. The Sunday School teachers could lead in the prayer session. Visitors, or those who do not attend Sunday School, could assemble in the sanctuary or another class of their choice. If the Sunday School teacher is absent, encourage the assistant or another person to direct the prayer time.

- A prayer bulletin is most beneficial. The pastor, or someone he designates, could prepare the bulletin on the afternoon of the mid-week service. The pastor's sermon outline could be printed. Prayer requests could be listed, such as the sick, the college students, the names of missionaries, specific church needs, etc., with a few spaces for added requests.

Fruitful praying demands preparation, usually on the part of the pastor. His goal should be to accomplish as much as possible in the time allotted. The prayer requests should include not just praying for the sick, but other requests that are important for the local church and around the world. Prepared materials to be placed in the hands of those in attendance can encourage more people to pray. Furthermore, those requests will be taken home to be remembered throughout the week.

Some churches prepare a large prayer bulletin board that is rolled out each mid-week service. The names of the missionaries the church supports, college students, servicemen or women, church projects, etc. are permanent requests. Other requests are added and taken off from week to week.

Every now and then, a different type of prayer meeting could be scheduled. For instance, plan a praise meeting rather than a prayer meeting. Spend the entire time praising the Lord. Entertain no requests. The pastor should have a long list of items for which to praise the Lord to add to the list that comes from the congregation. Also, the pastor could prepare slips of paper that state verses of thanksgiving. Pass out the paper in the offering plate. Those who take a verse could loudly read the verse, making any comments of thanksgiving. The meeting could conclude with several rendering prayers of thanksgiving.

Sad to say, prayer meetings may not be the most popular of our church services. However, the young pastor, as well as all pastors, are challenged to work at making the mid-week hour truly a spiritual oasis in the middle of the week. Church members laboring in the secular workforce need this spiritual uplift. The mid-week prayer meeting will provide that blessing to assist the born again believer in finishing the rest of the week in personal victory.

DON'T ROB YOUR CHURCH MEMBERS OF A BLESSING

Several older ladies and one man gladly went to Sunday School early. They gathered on the front church pew for one main job — fold the church bulletins. For years they had assumed this responsibility. Probably an hour or more before anyone arrived, those faithful church members neatly folded every bulletin. The vital means of communication were stacked, ready for the ushers to easily distribute before the morning services.

Only once or twice did I get to the church building early enough to observe this faithful crew eagerly performing their self-appointed responsibility. Very few of those who met for worship really knew who provided this personal care to the weekly pages of announcements.

Since we also produced a church newsletter, funds became available to purchase a paper folder. This piece of office equipment surely saved time. The office staff was excited. "Let's fold the bulletins, too," declared a secretary. A good idea, I thought.

So, the next Sunday the folded bulletins were placed on the usher's table. I told one of the dear saints that their services would no longer be needed. Case closed! Not a single one of those volunteers ever complained or criticized me. They could have. They should have!

You see, young preacher, I robbed those faithful few of performing the only job they did in that church. Later I apologized. The wrongdoing was confessed to the Lord. But, I also learned a lesson, I hope. Don't take away a responsibility of a faithful church member who is doing a good job.

Some Of The Best Help
Some of the best help comes from the hands of the senior saints. Not only fold bulletins, but this special group can perform a variety of jobs around the church. They can open and close the church buildings, attach labels to mailings, make telephone calls to advertise special church services, and cut off postage stamps from envelopes for missionary projects. Their schedules allow them to cut the church grass, trim the bushes, wash the windows, and even clean the church building.

Waiting To Be Asked
Most seniors are just waiting to be asked. A young preacher should make a list of church jobs that need to be done. Determine how many of those jobs can be performed by a senior citizen. Ask the older person to pray about the opportunity. You just may be pleasantly surprised at how much church work can be accomplished by "volunteers who are drafted."

Provide Recognition
The older church members deserve to be recognized. Often they have faithfully served in years past. Sponsor "Senior Sundays." Recognize everyone above a certain age with a small gift. Maybe the church could provide a special luncheon for this elect group.

Have an "eighty's club?' or a "seventy's club" of those in the church family who are of that age and above. Let them select their favorite songs one Sunday. On their birthday, give them the opportunity of testifying or selecting the congregational songs or reading the Scripture. Just make them feel important.

It was my honor to have two former pastors in one of my pastorates. The duet sat together on the second row. The "amens" from their feeble lips put fire in my sermons. To ask the one who could sing to render a solo on a Sunday evening even though the hymn book almost shook out of his hands, put a sparkle in his eyes. Both loved to fill the pulpit in my absence or on special occasions. At times I would take them to revival meetings, church conferences, or visiting in the homes. What a blessing these veteran preachers proved to be to my ministry.

Seek Wisdom
Young preacher, lean on the wisdom of an older man in your congregation. Find the man that displays trust and faith in the Lord, one who has been in the church many years. Go to him to discuss plans you have for the church. Seek his counsel when you are facing difficult people in the congregation. Request his prayer support. Pray with him.

Female Saints

Also, find a female saint in the congregation that you know prays regularly. One morning I went to the study, eagerly anticipating a fruitful day. An annoying telephone call and a disgruntled employee got my day off to a terrible start. About 9 A.M. I told the secretary that I was leaving and did not know when I was returning. Getting in my car and driving up and down several streets, I didn't know what to do. Praying for guidance, the Lord seemed to lead me to the home of a widow who lived alone. She hesitantly invited me in that early in the morning. I sat in her presence and listened to her reveal how two of her children and her husband died. She did not shed a tear but rejoiced in the Lord's provisions. I found a precious saint. Before leaving her home, this dear believer prayed for her pastor. This older woman's prayer support was sought when I needed a special touch from heaven. It was so refreshing to hear her voice utter blessings upon her pastor.

Valuable Church Members

Young preacher, some of the most valuable members of your congregation are those in pain, gripped by arthritis, covered with wrinkles, and often feeling useless. Run with the teens, play with the juniors, meet with the church officers, but, by all means, seek the counsel and pray with the senior saints. Many of these jewels will share wisdom with you that is so necessary.

SHOULD YOU CONDUCT A RADIO BROADCAST?

Radio is still a very effective method of communicating the gospel of Jesus Christ. Especially in some communities, the local radio station is eagerly listened to by the citizens. Radio not only allows for the presentation of Biblical truths, but the programs inform the community of the pastor's personality and the church's programs.

If you are really interested in conducting this type of outreach ministry, may I make some suggestions, based on many years of producing radio programs?

Seek The Wisdom Of Others
A pastor who has conducted a radio ministry could give you valuable information on the value, methods, problems, challenges, and support of a radio ministry. Be willing to travel to a pastor's office or make a telephone call to seek his wisdom.

Contact The Station
In conjunction with the radio station manager, the length of the program, the days and the time must be determined. Programs that are presented when people are traveling to and from work are ideal. Securing a slot just before or after the news could be most effective. Sign a contract. Be clear about the cost and the method of payment.

Determine The Length Of The Program
Five minute programs will demand more preparation time. Ten or fifteen minute programs would be easier to present since a preacher could use material he has previously preached. Also, will music be a part of the program? Music demands much more preparation time and more equipment.

How Will The Program Be Sustained Financially?
Sometimes the church will include this ministry in the budget. Other preachers take on this as a personal project. Occasionally advertising can pay for the time. But, don't depend upon the listening audience to support the programs financially in most cases. The radio station must be paid on time. If a bill gets over two months behind and you are responsible, personally borrow the money, pay the station and discontinue the ministry.

Prepare Well
Radio preachers shouldn't stutter or repeat themselves when radio time is costing two or three dollars every minute. Heart and mind preparations are essential when the preacher sits behind a microphone and preaches to an unseen audience. The first few years of broadcasting,

I studied a book of the Bible and wrote down every word to be spoken. Church members then typed the manuscripts. Therefore, triple blessings were bestowed, first upon me, then the radio listener, and then the typist. Also, radio programs should not include information that "dates" the broadcast. Prepare each recording with the intention of using it again.

Offer Literature?
Booklets can be purchased in bulk quantities and offered on the radio programs. Usually literature on the family will be requested more than any other subject. However, don't depend upon this to pay the radio bill. Postage will often cost more than the literature. Many people who write will not send any money. Plus, unless you have some help from a church member or a secretary, preparing materials for mailing can be extremely time consuming. Count the cost before you get involved in offering literature. Most listeners never write. I read that one person out of one thousand listeners will write. That figure may be fairly accurate. If the literature and postage are paid for, you could offer the materials to listeners who request by a telephone call or an e-mail.

Is This Ministry Fruitful?
A lady in our town, parked her vehicle on the shoulder of the road and prayed the sinner's prayer to trust Christ as personal Savior after hearing a pastor preaching on a radio program. A family from Puerto Rico, visiting in the Williamsburg, Virginia, area, heard my Saturday morning broadcast and accepted the invitation to attend our Sunday morning church service. A former pastor was preaching. The man and woman accepted Christ as Savior at the church altar. They returned that same day

to their home via airplane. I wrote a missionary in that area and they attended that mission church.

Benefit The Church?
Sometimes people will visit the church of a radio preacher. Often they attend just one service. Maybe they want to see if he is tall, short, fat, or thin! In some areas, the radio program will attract a few prospects for salvation or church membership. But, radio also attracts some peculiar people, like the man who wants to tell you what to preach (and it takes him two hours to explain), or the people who send you anonymous letters, cassette tapes, and booklets to set you straight on some doctrine. If the young preacher thinks he can build a strong church through his radio broadcast, think again. Radio is really a missionary ministry. The seed is planted and the radio preacher trusts the Lord to bear spiritual fruit.

Still Convinced!
Good. Purchase a quality recorder after discussing with the radio station manager the type he recommends. Purchase the tapes or discs. Pray. Study. Prepare. Take the recorded material to the radio station. Trust God for the results. May you experience spiritual fruit from this ministry.

SHOULD I ESTABLISH A CHRISTIAN SCHOOL?

The young preacher could possibly find himself in a community that seems to be fertile ground for establishing a Christian school. Church members may petition an alternative to the public school or another community educational program. Possibly a burden to plant a church school becomes overwhelming as the Scriptures are read. Maybe a sermon is heard about the mandate for Christian education.

Whatever the reason for even considering to establish a Christian school, the young preacher must bathe this project with much prayer. Counsel from other ministers and church leaders involved in Christian education should be sought.

After prayer and fasting, if this burden continues, the preacher is now faced with one of the greatest challenges of his ministry. If God is in it, the pathway will be made clear. The burden will produce action. The action will set into motion the planting of a Christian school.

Get Church Support
Too many educational endeavors have been established by a pastor who had a burden but failed to share that burden with his congregation. Discuss this idea with the deacons. Share the proposed project with the church board. Lead the church into voting to establish a Christian school.

Borrow Brains
That's what Bob Jones, Sr. did when he established Bob Jones University. Most pastors do not have the academic background to properly establish a church-sponsored school. That does not mean that the pastor cannot initiate this project. But, it does mean that he absolutely must lean on the wisdom and direction of others who have the knowledge and experience,

Determine The Rules
A church-sponsored school should be distinctively different. The rules, standards, guidelines that make it unique must be recorded in a handbook to be distributed to students and parents. Don't belittle other schools to exalt your educational endeavor. Just be determined to lay the foundation for a quality, above the average, Christ-exalting educational program.

How Many Grades?
Just kindergarten the first year and add a grade each year is what some schools have done. Maybe kindergarten through grade three would be a better beginning. Determine from the community and church what is actually needed.

Curriculum

This decision demands much home work. Visit schools that use different programs. Compare the different courses of study. Seek guidance from pastors and principals. This decision will affect the school greatly. It may determine the success or failure of the school.

Finances

Many church-sponsored schools do not charge a sufficient tuition to provide for the many costs of operating a school. Quality education is worth the cost. Also, tuition must provide an adequate salary provision for the principal and teachers. Ask at least a dozen established church schools to send you their tuition and salary scale.

Secure Teachers

Visit Christian colleges to find qualified, dedicated teachers. Search your church for teachers who may want to invest their abilities and experience in this new educational project. Once the teachers are secured, provide a continued education for them by taking the teachers to one or two of the national or regional educational meetings every year.

Stay With The Ministry

Don't begin a church school, resign the church, and leave inexperienced workers holding the bag. The pastor should be the overseer; however, a principal or qualified supervisors should be prepared to conduct the operation on a daily basis. And, young pastor, pray for patience. School students dirty walls, stain carpet, wear out pews, break equipment, and trample on shrubbery. Church members may hold you accountable!

Rewards?
Yes, Christian education is rewarding. The purpose of a church sponsoring a Christian school is evangelism, edification, and education. Parents (as well as students) can be won to the Lord. Students can be trained in the ways of the Lord. And, of course, the school should excel in providing a quality education for all students. So, young preacher, don't jump in this arena quickly. But, if the Lord leads, jump in with both feet and hands. Use your head and heart to prepare boys and girls to live in this world as salt and light, as Matthew 5:13 and 14 declare. Eternity will reveal the true results.

OPERATING A CHURCH SCHOOL

The young preacher may inherit a church school, or he may help establish one. Principal and teachers must be qualified spiritually and academically in order to produce quality education in a Christian environment.
Here are some suggestions in operating the school with efficiency and progress.

Meet
Meet with the principal at a specific time each week for prayer. While meetings to discuss the school's operation are vital, prayer time is even more important.

Schedule
Schedule a regular prayer time with teachers and staff. Perhaps half of the group could meet for 15 minutes Tuesday and Thursday mornings before teachers are due in their classes. The other half could meet Wednesday and Friday. They should meet even if you are out of town.

Be Generous
Be generous to your school personnel. Recognize their birthdays with a card (mailed through the postal service). Use the bulletin board in the office or teachers' workroom to place a picture of the Teacher-of-the-Week.

Put small gifts in the teachers' boxes occasionally: red-leaded pencil, booklets, letters of commendation, coupons to a restaurant, etc.

Arrange
Arrange for the entire school family to eat together at least twice a year. If the school can't afford to take them to a restaurant, then schedule a potluck supper.

Give
Give them a Christmas bonus. Provide a financial gift at the end of the year if surplus funds exist.

Visit
Visit each classroom occasionally. Sit in the back of the room and observe the class. It benefits both pupils and teachers.

Pray
Pray regularly from the pulpit for the principal, teachers and school. Always be available to counsel or pray with any teacher. Never reveal the nature of their problem or prayer request.

Attend
Attend school conventions with the principal and teachers. Stay for the entire program. Allow your wife to attend with you.

Provide
Provide adequate financial provisions and benefits. Get personally involved in raising salary and benefits.

Speak

Speak in chapel regularly. Speak to the students on how to respect and show kindness to teachers. Deliver salvation messages. Give invitations. Challenge the students from the book of Proverbs.

Use

Use the school to minister to souls who will live somewhere forever. The school can produce eternal benefits.

HOW TO TREAT THE GUEST PREACHER

Many churches still sponsor Bible Conferences, Revival Meetings, Missionary Conferences, and Special Days. These activities usually require at least one guest speaker. Sometimes the invited speaker is left to "fend" for himself. Adequate housing and hospitality would reflect a better testimony for the church. Let me make some suggestions on how to treat the guest speaker.

Promote
Requesting a preacher or missionary to visit your church demands his or her time, efforts, preparation, and prayer. The very least the young preacher can do is to advertise the special meeting. Most newspapers will accept news articles. Some will even print a picture of the guest speaker. Radio and television stations will provide spot promotions at times. A letter or card to local pastors announcing the meeting could be beneficial. Neatly printed brochures or handbills could be used. In other words, promote the meeting with effective advertising.

Prepare The Congregation
Weeks ahead of the meeting announce the upcoming services in the bulletin. Provide interesting information about the speaker. Show the church members a recent picture. Be enthusiastic about the speaker's abilities and

gifts, but, of course, don't exaggerate. Over promotion of the speaker can dampen the spirits of the congregation.

Pray Fervently
First, the young preacher should set aside specific times for personally praying for the preacher and the services. Call people's names before the Lord who need a special touch from the Lord during the meeting. Then, call the church to prayer. Remind the congregation of the meeting several weeks ahead during the mid-week service. Ask the congregation to pray at the church altar or in small groups for the speaker and the special meeting. Call on church leaders to pray audibly for the speaker. Maybe cottage prayer meetings, all-night prayer sessions, extended mid- week prayer meetings, personal fasting and praying times, and even a week of prayer would greatly benefit the meeting. And, young preacher, be sure to pray with the guest speaker. Pray in the church sanctuary at least during the day. Anoint the speaker in prayer before and after the services. A group of men praying with the speaker just before the services would be most encouraging.

Plan Adequately
If the visiting speaker is going to stay in a motel, arrange to have a fruit, cracker, and soft drink basket placed in the room before he or she arrives. If the guest is diabetic, be sure to make the beverages diet and the crackers sugar free. Arrange to feed the special speaker only two large meals a day. Maybe a late breakfast and an early evening meal would be adequate. If the guest is staying in a home, alert the family about a proper eating schedule. Often over eating will make the preacher or missionary too full to function satisfactorily.

Pay The Speaker Well

Full-time evangelists surely need more than a pastor who is drawing a salary from a church. A good guideline for all speakers would be one-hundred dollars a service plus mileage (whatever the federal allowance is) either from the church budget or love offerings. For the evangelist, maybe the last night a special love offering could be received. The believers should be challenged to give a generous offering to the evangelist who usually does not have a set salary provision. Give your congregation the opportunity to practice Galatians 6:6 *("Let him that is taught in the word communicate unto him that teacheth in all good things.")*

Missionaries should receive generous love offerings plus pledges of monthly support. The pastor is probably the leader in these matters, encouraging and challenging the congregation. He should not be selfish or jealous. If the young preacher takes care of other men of God then the Lord will provide for his needs. And, whatever is received in the offerings each night or the special offering should go to the guest speaker. It would be dishonest to announce that the offering goes to the speaker and then the church pocket some for the general fund.

Preserve The Decisions

It is usually the young preacher's responsibility to train counselors when decisions are made at the altar. Church members should be available to meet with those who make decisions. Proper follow up literature, decisions cards and pens, and a box of tissues should be near the pulpit. Those who make decisions for Christ would benefit from a pastoral visit immediately. A discipleship

class should be established, taught by the pastor or a trained associate. Church members could be assigned to visit the new converts.

Ponder The Fruit
Immediately after the special services, write the guest speaker a note of appreciation, present an optimistic report in the bulletin, report the results to church newspapers, schedule a baptismal service, write a letter of challenge to those who made decisions, and begin to plan for the next meeting. Good meetings don't always produce large crowds. One decision for Christ, one young person who yields to enroll in a Christian college, one backslider who confesses, one church member who begins to tithe — these, plus many more decisions, prove that conducting a special meeting was worth all of the effort.

HOW TO CONDUCT A BUSINESS MEETING

"Without counsel purposes are disappointed: but in the multitude of counselors they are established"
(Proverbs 15:22).

One challenging responsibility for the pastor is the church business meeting. While more preachers die of heartache than heart attack, business meeting pressures may make you think otherwise. The pastor can eliminate much of the pressure. Here's how:

Be Prepared
After you arrive at a new pastorate, discuss how the church conducts its business meetings with the deacons, church clerk, or older member. Learn all you can about the church's methods of operation. Visit a veteran church member and ask him about the history of the church. Refuse to listen to gossip or disparaging remarks about former ministers or present church members.

Make No Immediate Changes
Win the confidence of the membership before trying to make changes in the manner the body has conducted church business. Discuss with the deacons how the

church conducts the business of the church. Just listen. Take notes. Promise nothing.

Plan Ahead
Map out a meeting strategy. Determine what business should be conducted by seeking counsel from a board member, deacon, or clerk. If a board meets before the actual church meeting, prepare an agenda for that meeting. Begin with prayer; conclude with prayer after prayer requests are given.

Put Everything On Paper
Budget proposals, nominations for office, large expenditures should be clearly stated on paper. Take personal notes. File them under business meetings.

Let The Majority Decide
Do not try to ramrod items through. Present business items clearly; ask for a motion and a second; allow time for discussion; and call for a vote. You may want to have prayer before you vote. Conclude with prayer after the business meeting ends, maybe around the alter. If the business decision could be decisive, ask for a motion to table the item for one week. Encourage the congregation to pray that week about the matter.

Avoid Unnecessary Business
Do not bring items before the church that may have been handled in a budget or a previous vote. Don't talk too much. Being nervous at the business meeting may cause the pastor to ramble, say too much, and confuse the issue.

Keep People Informed
Remember, informed church members conduct the Lord's business more efficiently. Use the bulletin and newsletter to keep them informed before and after business sessions about items of importance.

Control Yourself
Don't get angry and say something you will regret later. *"He that is slow to anger is better than the mighty; and he that ruleth his spirit than he that taketh a city."* Be patient. Take deep breaths. Pray. Remember that the church you pastor was "their church" long before you arrived. And, it will be "their church" long after you are gone.

MAKE MISSIONARY CONFERENCE A BLESSING

Good missionary meetings don't just happen. The pastor is the key to a successful conference. His attitude, promotion, and support set the pace for the congregation's response to missions. A well-planned missionary conference will benefit the church. God blesses the missions-minded church with more growth and spiritual stability.

Schedule A Missionary Conference
Schedule a missionary conference with several missionaries or just one missionary. Other churches in your area may cooperate in scheduling a conference.

The Name
Call the meetings "Missionary Revival Services" or a similar name. Words such as "conference" or "seminar" may scare some people from attending.

Order Literature
Distribute prayer cards and missions information in the bulletin several weeks before the conference begins. Ask a talented church member to develop a bulletin board with the pictures of the missionaries.

Plan Ahead
Form committees: advertising, hospitality, displays, etc. Mention the meetings from the pulpit with excitement and enthusiasm.

Show A Missionary Film
Show a film the week before the conference. (*Beyond The Gates Of Splendor* or *Beyond The Night* are excellent.)

Conduct Cottage Prayer Meetings
Encourage cottage prayer meetings the week before the conference. Pray for the special services, the missionaries by name, the family members of the missionaries, their safety of travel, their health, etc.

Arrange Accommodations
Arrange accommodations for the missionary or missionaries well in advance. Put flowers and a fruit basket in their motel room. Encourage your congregation to have them in their homes for a meal.

Don't Just Schedule Meetings
Do something special, for example:

- Conduct a poster contest for the children.
- Schedule special music.
- Plan an international banquet.
- Schedule a question and answer session.
- Invite local citizens of foreign nationality, especially those from the same country where the missionary serves.

- Distribute a mission's quiz, based on information about the missionaries and their different ministries, at the beginning of the conference.
- Discuss it the week after the services.

Allow The Missionary 45-60 Minutes
Allow adequate time for his presentation. Give him or her two services, if possible. Try to schedule just a few minutes for preliminaries. Take up the offering after the missionary speaks. Give all of the special offering to the missionary or mail a check to his account.

Encourage Financial Support
Encourage the congregation to support the missionaries and missions programs through the faith-promise plan or the church budget. Conduct a Faith-Promise Rally the last night of the services, challenging church members to personally support a missionary or missionaries above their tithe.

Follow Up
Follow up by reporting to the missionaries the results of the meetings. Preach missionary messages. Challenge young people to accept the call of missions. Pray for laborers.

WHAT IF YOU'RE VOTED OUT?

Some young preachers are often called to a church that has the history of not keeping pastors very long. My first pastorate terminated after just six months. Then, I had to stay there almost three months. Here are some principles I learned through the influence of God's Word, my wife, and an older pastor.

Accept The Fact
Accept the fact that you must leave. You may not consider it God's will, but be satisfied that the church has spoken and that you must abide by the decision.

Be Kind
Lashing out at those who want you to leave will accomplish nothing. Ask the Lord to give you a kind spirit.

Contact
Contact fellow pastors and other leaders to inform them of your leaving. Pastor friends can inform churches of your availability.

Continue
Continue to function as pastor. Visit the sick with a spiritual purpose, not to discuss why you were voted out. Pray and study faithfully. Don't sit home and pout.

Stay Optimistic
Stay optimistic around your wife and children. A move is more difficult on them than you. Assure them that God will open the right door in His own timing.

Do Not Speak Critically
Do not speak critically of church members. Do not try to settle church problems from the pulpit. Preach the Word of God as effectively as possible.

Study
Study the life of Christ during this time of crisis. Preach all your messages from this study. Exalt Christ in the pulpit.

Evaluate
Evaluate opportunities that come to you. An open door does not always mean you should walk through it. Better to work at a secular job a few months than accept the wrong pastorate.

Leave
Leave the church gracefully. Be kind, even to those who may not be kind to you or your family. Thank them publicly for the good things they have done. Write thank you notes (send them by the postal service) for gifts that are given.

Be Sure
Be sure that all bills are paid in the community. If necessary, borrow money from a bank and pay off all local debts.

Remember
Remember that the way you leave the church may determine your future ministry. If you love them in spite of your hurt and disappointment, they will remember your kind spirit.

If You Have Been Wronged
If you have been wronged, remember that the Lord exercises vengeance, not you. The congregation will remember your attitude. Teach church members how to accept this experience by your actions.

Dennis P. Wiggs
Especially For The Young Preacher

HOW TO LEAVE A PASTORATE

Today pastors are staying longer at a church. But, eventually every pastorate must come to a conclusion. Many reasons prevail for departing from ministering at a certain church: death, disability, resignation, retiring, losing a confidence vote, or being asked to leave. Often leaving a pastorate is not pleasant for the pastor, his family, and many in the congregation. When the spiritual leader finds it necessary to leave a congregation, whatever the reason, many times scars develop that affect some for many years. I believe the young preacher owes it to himself, his family, and the church family to leave with as little fanfare as possible.

Leave Graciously
Just out of seminary, I pastored a country church that accepted me as its first full-time pastor. The previous pastor had been instrumental in leading many to Christ in that church and his other half-time pastorate. The Lord blessed the ministry from the very first service when a young man trusted Christ as Savior and soon enrolled in a Christian college. A strong youth group was quickly developed. I was enjoying the first fruits of an active ministry. But, after six months the deacons announced to me that in March of each year the church "voted on the

pastor." I yielded without any question. My wife, our son, and I went to a rented home while the congregation cast the votes. About the time we walked into our four room dwelling, a deacon dialed our telephone number and announced abruptly, "Well, you lost!" I exclaimed, "Lost, what does that mean?" "You got three months to find another church," the deacon declared and concluded the telephone conversation. My wife and I were dumbfounded. We just couldn't believe that our six-month church honeymoon was ending in such a manner. An older minister who performed our wedding ceremony gave this shocked young preacher some sound advice. "Dennis, don't try to take care of your grief from the pulpit. Just preach Jesus!" Good counsel which I tried to follow for almost three months.

Young preacher, when the congregation decides for you to leave, don't try to "straighten out the problems." Preach Jesus. Pray and then pray some more. And, leave as graciously as possible. By the way, that church that decided for me to leave after six months has called me back for revival meetings, funerals, weddings, and other events. Because I practiced the advice of the older minister, I can return to that church without shame or embarrassment.

Leave Carefully
Be sure every bill is paid, even if you must borrow the money from a lending institution. Seek to have a good relationship with everyone, regardless of what they may have done to you. Prepare the way for the next pastor. Try to leave a sweet taste in all of the church members' mouths when your name is mentioned. Leave the parsonage spotlessly cleaned. Return every single item

you may have borrowed. Keep paying your tithe to the church until your last pay check. These suggestions may sound like compromising. Not true. Remember, you are a man of God.

Act that role. You may need that church someday or that congregation may need you. Leave with the door cracked open for future opportunities to minister to that group of people.

Leave Lovingly
Surely young preachers (and older preachers, too) find it necessary to depart from a ministry that they do not want to leave. A forced exit is usually quite bitter. Hard feelings can develop. Church members, even preachers, can say words they really don't mean. The forced out preacher and those who force him out can possess ill will. Young preacher, do your very best to love those people who "turn against you." Most of them are truly born again, even though they may not demonstrate the part. In fact, most church members just don't know how to terminate a pastor's ministry. Many of them work in a secular atmosphere where hiring and firing are acted out without compassion. That worldly attitude often flows over into the church without the membership even realizing what is happening. So, brother, just love those people. Maybe through this agonizing experience of your leaving, this church may be able to mature into better believers. Possibly they can learn at your expense how to deal more lovingly with the next pastor.

Leave
Whatever the reason you leave a church, be sure to leave. Refrain from speaking despairingly about some in the

congregation. The next pastor just may be able to lead them on to greater spiritual heights. (And, don't be jealous!) Refuse to call back on Sunday nights to a favorite church member to ask how the services went that day. Turn a deaf ear to what is happening at your previous pastorate. Unless absolutely necessary, don't immediately return for funerals and weddings. Divorce yourself from that pastorate. Set your aspirations and affections on a new ministry.

FORMS

USE FORMS

The young preacher will be called upon to respond repeatedly to specific requests that demand a decision. Rather than handle each request every time it surfaces, develop certain forms that provide answers that help make your decision easier. Let me give just a few suggestions. I'm sure you can develop other forms that apply to your own local ministry.

The Marriage Questionnaire
When engaged couples (or their parents) come to you requesting that you conduct the wedding, place in their hands the Marriage Questionnaire. This procedure will help save time when you set up the first counseling session. The couple will also get a hint of your position on weddings. Furthermore, by filing the questionnaire you will have needed information at your fingertips before and after the wedding.

For example, the questionnaire could ask the full names of the engaged couple, the addresses, telephone numbers, and the names of the parents. However, the most valuable questions would ask how long they have dated, have they been married before, and why they want to marry each other. The questions also provide you the tool of establishing Biblical and moral principles by asking if dancing will be encouraged at the reception, will alcoholic beverages be served, and other pertinent questions.

Then, in the questionnaire, certain statements could be made in regards to the fees, cleaning up of the church and fellowship hall, and other items that possibly engaged couples would not consider.

Several counseling sessions before the wedding are advisable. This questionnaire could be used to record your notes made during these sessions. Of course, all of this material should be filed for future reference.

The Baptismal Form
Besides providing some basic, Biblical guidelines for baptism, this form should record the full name, address, birth date, and sex of the one to be baptized. The information gleaned from this form assists you in recording the necessary items to include in the certificate and in the records to be kept by the church. A file of all baptized believers should be sustained in a place of safe keeping. Baptismal certificates are appreciated by most of those who are baptized.

Church Member's Form
A means for church members to provide valuable information to the pastor can benefit the operation of a church. This form can be distributed in the church bulletin over a period of a month. The information should be stored in a computer or in a notebook. The

questionnaire should list the church member's full name, sex, address, birth date, telephone number, place of employment, children, and their birthdates. Every couple or three years this information may have to be updated.

Death Request Form
When pastors preach on death and the consequences of death, this is a good time to mention wills, written requests, methods of burial (embalming or cremation), etc. A form could be provided for the church member to list suggestions for funeral services that would benefit the pastor, church musicians, and family members at the death of this individual. Funeral homes often provide excellent materials on this subject.

Spiritual Concern Form
Providing a small form for church members to indicate the name or names of the unconverted is beneficial to the pastor and his outreach ministry. This questionnaire should not only include the name, sex, age, and address of someone who is an unbeliever, but it may be wise to ask the church member if he or she has witnessed to this prospect. This form could be distributed several times a year to secure the names of the unsaved.

Decision Form
When someone goes to the church altar for a salvation decision or to join the church, it would be most helpful to the pastor if a basic form and a pen or pencil were placed in the hands of the decision maker. Maybe a deacon or a church clerk could be assigned the responsibility of making sure this form is filled out and given to the pastor immediately after the church service.

Benevolent Form

Often the pastor is called upon to assist people with finances to pay house rent, buy food, and other needs. Rather than field every call without adequate information, a Benevolent Form can be extremely helpful. Before the one asking for help (this is primarily for those outside of your church) is given an interview, request the person to give information such as full name, address, age, sex, health, place of employment, spouse's name, children and their ages. Then, expect the person to write on the form the request and why. It would be ideal if this form could be provided by a church secretary before the person is interviewed. After the form is completed, then you (or the deacons) can interview the person. Often this form will scare away people who are attempting to take advantage of the church.

These forms may be copied.

MARRIAGE QUESTIONNAIRE

Date _____

Name of prospective bride _____

Present address _____
_____

Telephone _____

Name of father _____

Address _____
_____

Name of mother _____

Address _____
_____

Name of prospective groom _____

Present address _____
_____

Telephone _____

Name of father _____

Address _____

_____

Name of mother _____

Address _____

_____

Wedding date _____ Time _____

Place _____

Minister _____

Telephone _____

Address _____

_____

How long have you been engaged? _____

Have you been married before? Man _____ Woman_____

Man: Are you a born again Christian? ___ Explain ____

_____

_____

Church membership: _____

Pastor _____ Telephone _____

Woman: Are you a born again Christian? _____

Explain _____

_____

Church membership: _____

Pastor _____ Telephone _____

Would you consent to two pre-marital counseling sessions?

Man _____ Woman _____

Director of wedding _____

Address _____

Telephone _____

Musicians _____

_____

_____

Wedding party names _____

_____

_____

Music to be sung or played in wedding (only sacred music is appropriate):_____

_____

_____

Being that this is a church wedding, alcoholic beverages should not be served at the rehearsal supper or wedding reception. Agree? _____

The wedding party members should dress modestly for the rehearsal and wedding.
Agree? _____

BAPTISMAL FORM

Name _____

Address _____

_____

Telephone _____ Birthdate _____ Age _____

School you attend _____

Occupation _____

Parent's Names _____

Parent's Telephone Numbers_____

When did you accept Jesus Christ as your personal Savior?_____

Describe what you did when you trusted Christ. _____
_____
_____
_____
_____
_____
_____

Please return to pastor before you are baptized.

REQUEST FOR FUNDS

Today's Date and Time _____

Name _____

Address _____

_____

Telephone _____

Date of Birth _____

Name of Spouse _____

Ages of Children _____

Last employment _____

Social Security Number _____

Have you requested funds from Social Services? _____

Reason for the request for funds _____

_____

_____

_____

The amount of money you need? _____

The above facts are true _____

                            Please sign your name

Your request for funds will be decided by the church deacons. They may visit your home before the decision is made.

CHURCH FAMILY INFORMATION

Please fill out this form to assist the pastor in ministering at this church.

Name _____

Telephone Number _____

Address _____

_____

E-Mail Address _____

Date of Birth_____

Employment _____

Marital Information _____

Name of Spouse _____

Birthdate _____

Anniversary _____

Employment _____

Children's names and dates of birth:
_____
_____
_____
_____

INFORMATION WHEN I DIE

Please place this in your Bible or will. You may want to give it to the funeral director.

Name _____

Date of Birth _____

Funeral Home Requested _____

Burial Location _____

Minister Requested_____

Musicians Requested _____

Music Requested_____

Scripture Requested _____

_____

I understand that these are only requests. I do trust that my family and/or the funeral director will try to carry out these requests as near as possible.

Signed _____

Date _____

CHILD DEDICATION
-Sample-

The parents of _____

and _____ assemble

today to dedicate this precious child to the Lord.

_____ was born _____ at

_____ Hospital.

Her/his parents were partners in delivering this beautiful child. The Psalmist declared in Psalm 139, "*I will praise thee, for I am fearfully and wonderfully made: marvelous are thy works ...*" We rejoice with _____ _____ and _____ for the birth of this child.

This couple is to be commended for their commitment in dedicating this lovely child. They are following the pattern established by Simeon who resided in the temple in Jerusalem waiting for the coming of the Christ Child. Simeon took Jesus in his arms and blessed God by declaring that Jesus had been born for a specific purpose. Today, we praise God for _____'s birth. We lift her/him to heaven. We commit this little one into the Lord's hands to provide direction to the parents in the rearing and training, and, we pray, the salvation of this child.

First, I admonish the parents to rear _____ in the ways of the Lord. Psalm 127:3 declares that "*Lo, children are an heritage of the Lord: and the fruit of the womb is his*

reward." Proverbs 22:6 promises, "*Train up a child in the way he should go: and when he is old, he will not depart from it."*

The responsibility and privilege of child rearing lie in the hands of the parents. God will hold this couple accountable for training their child the right way. And what is the right way? I believe that proper training includes family devotions, faithful church attendance, daily discipline, and abounding love and Biblical examples. This child was born with a sinful nature, as is true with all of us. She/he will need much prayer. She/he will learn how to live by observing the lives of these parents. I challenge this father and mother to point their child to the Lord Jesus Christ who can save her/his soul and become a child of God.

Secondly, the grandparents must love without showing partiality. They should be aware of little eyes watching and yearning to follow the example set by the grandparents. Proverbs 13:22 declares that "*A good man leaveth an inheritance to his children's children.*" The best inheritance is not financial or earthly goods, but the spiritual examples that this child will long remember, even after grandparents have deceased.

Thirdly, this congregation should dedicate themselves in assisting these parents in rearing their child in the proper way. Some of you will be her/his teachers. All of you will either set a good or not so good example. This child and the parents need your prayer support. Please don't invite _____ into your homes and expose his/her innocent mind to the things of the world. Please refuse to allow this child to hear you speaking despairingly of

others. Invite her/him into your hearts for you to love, challenge, and encourage.

So, we dedicate the parents, the grandparents, the congregation, and this pastor to influence this child in the perfect ways of the Lord. We surrender ourselves to be a blessing rather than a curse, a challenge rather than a condemnation, and an encouragement rather than a discouragement.

Let us pray. Father, we are grateful for the marriage of this couple, _____ and _____. We thank you for the conception of _____, the natural birth, this blessing, this dedication, and this opportunity to direct the paths of this child down the pathway of life. Please give this couple wisdom, patience, love, and strength to daily mold her/him after the Scriptures. We pray that _____ will trust Christ as Savior early in life, be baptized, unite with the church, and serve the Savior faithfully. We surrender _____ to you and pray your richest blessings upon this precious child. I pray in Jesus' name. Amen.

www.ingramcontent.com/pod-product-compliance
Lightning Source LLC
Chambersburg PA
CBHW060821050426
42453CB00008B/532